With much
Birthda

Mum & Dad.
x x x

PAISLEY –
A LIVERPOOL
LEGEND

by Stan Liversedge

British Library Cataloguing in Publication Data
A catalogue record of this book is available from the British Library
ISBN 0-947808-85-X

© Stan Liversedge and Soccer Book Publishing Ltd.
First published 1996

published in Great Britain by   Soccer Book Publishing Ltd.
                                       72 St. Peters Avenue
                                       Cleethorpes
                                       N.E. Lincolnshire
                                       DN35 8HU
                                       England

Printed in Great Britain by Redwood Books, Trowbridge, Wiltshire

CONTENTS

INTRODUCTION

Nobody Did it Better

NESSIE SHANKLY called them The Terrible Twins. They were her husband, Bill Shankly, and his sidekick, Bob Paisley. Two men who seemed to be as different as cheese and chalk and yet who, when paired together, lifted Liverpool Football Club to the pinnacle of achievement, both at home and abroad. Through the years that I knew both men, I gained the impression that there were occasions when Bob Paisley acted as a restraining influence upon Bill Shankly; and it was an impression which Nessie Shankly appeared to confirm, when people were eulogising Paisley at the time of his death.

Indeed, there came a day when, in the presence of many witnesses, myself included, Bill Shankly acknowledged that he felt a twinge of jealousy even as he paid Bob Paisley – by then his successor as manager of Liverpool Football Club, and as Manager of the Year – the tribute he so richly deserved. If Shankly was the man who set Liverpool on the road to glory, Paisley was the one who became hailed as the greatest manager British football has ever known – and that, remember, takes into account the deeds of such illustrious names as Sir Matt Busby, Alex Ferguson, Bill Nicholson, Jock Stein, Don Revie, Harry Catterick, Brian Clough and the Laird of Anfield himself, Bill Shankly. Yet never was there a more reluctant hero than Bob Paisley, the modest Geordie from the North-East pit village of Hetton-le-Hole.

I was privileged to be welcomed into the homes of both Matt Busby (whom I knew for more than 30 years) and Bob Paisley (whom I knew for around a quarter of a century), and in each case we talked football for hours as we also enjoyed a tot or two of whisky. There was no shortage of Scotch – in Paisley's own case especially, considering how many times he had been voted Bell's Manager of the Month (and Manager of the Year)! And as we talked, each man not only told me his story but, to a degree at any rate, felt able to confide in me.

Bill Shankly and Matt Busby were both Scots, and they hailed from the same area north of the border. In Alex Ferguson's day as manager at Manchester United, he made the point that Scots possessed the main ingredient for success as managers … a determination to be winners. A noted columnist made the point that when people thought of the successful managers, they tended to pick out the names of Scots such as Shankly, Busby, Stein and Ferguson. Yet Bob Paisley, the man from Geordieland, eclipsed anything so far achieved by any other manager in British football. Paisley himself offered the view that 'you don't even dream about it … I'm quite sure of that'. Sometimes you had to interpret what Bob meant, and on this occasion he was talking about management and the success it had brought him.

A fellow-Geordie, Lawrie McMenemy – who enjoyed F.A. Cup-final success with Southampton and experienced the other side of the coin with Sunderland – recalled the phrase 'a canny lad', and explained that in essence it meant 'a nice lad'. Bob Paisley was, without a doubt, a canny lad. When Bob went to Buckingham Palace to receive the OBE, McMenemy coined another phrase for it. Instead of the Order of the British Empire, he claimed it stood for 'Our Bob Excels'. He had won more monthly managerial awards than anyone else.

The relationship between the supporters of Liverpool and Manchester United has not always been the most cordial in football; the rivalry, indeed, has been so keen that many Liverpool fans would prefer their team to beat United ahead of giving Everton a hiding. But one of the most genuine tributes to Paisley came from United supporters when, like hundreds of thousands of others around the country, they observed a minute's silence for Bob before kick-off against Blackburn Rovers at Old Trafford. And it was Sir Bobby Charlton, a Geordie who became a United legend in his own lifetime, who paid another sincere tribute to the man who gave so much in the cause of Liverpool.

Charlton became a Mancunian by adoption, although he has never lost his North-East accent; likewise Paisley, who married a Liverpool lass, became a Liverpudlian by adoption, while preserving his Geordie accent. Charlton summed up Bob Paisley this way: 'He was a real football man. He was an honest man. There was no evil in him'. That was certainly true – though Bob Paisley had a streak of tempered steel in his make-up.

The Charlton verdict: 'He was from my part of the world, a North-Easterner, and he always made me welcome whenever I went to Anfield. He was a lovely, unforgettable man, and his deeds will never be surpassed, certainly not in my lifetime'. Two of the points Sir Bobby Charlton made were echoed by a man who knew Paisley better than most – Liverpool's chief executive, Peter Robinson, who recalled his honesty, as well as his immense knowledge of football. Robinson also went back to the days when the famous Anfield bootroom became established as part of footballing folklore.

In those days, Shankly was at the helm, and his backroom team included another Scot, Reuben Bennett, Bob Paisley and Joe Fagan. They were to be joined by the likes of Ronnie Moran, Tom Saunders and Roy Evans. Bennett was somewhat dour, and he had been a goalkeeper north of the border – indeed, he gained a reputation as the man who took the longest goal kick in history. The story went that he gave the ball such 'welly' that it sailed out of the ground, landed on the back of a lorry – and ended up in Carlisle.

Paisley, Fagan and Evans were to follow Shankly in the managerial hot seat at Liverpool, while Saunders – originally cast as the club's youth-development officer – graduated to the status of elder statesman and was appointed a director. Moran briefly tasted what it was like to pick the team, then he soldiered on as a member of the backroom staff … like Paisley, it seemed that he was satisfied to be of service to the club in virtually any capacity.

According to Peter Robinson, the bootroom was started by Bob Paisley and Joe Fagan with Shankly flitting in and out, while his henchmen passed many an hour after training and matches debating what had gone right and what had gone wrong. The bootroom became known as the place where visiting managers could expect a warm welcome after the match – usually their team had lost – and they were offered some liquid hospitality. The story went that one manager made his way to the bootroom after a Saturday game and imbibed generously – so much so, that on the team coach going home he gained sufficient Dutch courage to tell his chairman what he could do with his job.

One noted columnist, Richard Littlejohn, wrote that it took Paisley's death to remind people 'that when it came to winning trophies in style, he was peerless. Yet even at the peak of his career, I don't think I can ever remember anyone putting his name forward for the England job. Perhaps if he had worn sharp suits, had a profitable sideline as a TV pundit and run a night club, he might have been taken more seriously'. Well, I can remember the time when Bob Paisley did wear what, for him, might be termed 'a sharp suit' … it had been specially made by a tailor, and it was a darkish suit which had the Liverpool F.C. motif running through the stripes. True, you had to look fairly closely to spot the motif, but it was there, all right. When it came to Liverpool Football Club, Bob Paisley never liked to say No.

When it came to putting on the style, he preferred his team to strut their stuff – although that probably wasn't the phrase he would have used. Bob came across as an avuncular figure, a man who liked to be comfortable in woolly cardigan and carpet slippers, a man who went to work wearing a cloth cap. The Daily Mail's Patrick Collins termed Paisley 'a deeply private person … football was his game, Liverpool his club and Anfield his workplace. That was all the public needed to know. Had he been even marginally more extrovert, then the nation might have demanded that he be made manager of England. How he would have hated it. Much better to stay where he was known and lovingly appreciated, where he could nurture fine players, and where he could haul in oceans of silverware each and every year. For Bob Paisley did all that. And nobody has done it better'.

One by one, the famous names in football lined up to pay homage to Paisley, as his deeds were recalled and his memory revered. Liverpool manager Roy Evans, who hung up his playing boots when he was still in his mid-20's – 'that was a very difficult decision for me to make', he once told me – acknowledged that it was Paisley 'who pushed me into the coaching side of football'. Evans rated Bob 'one of the great people of Liverpool and the most successful man in the history of football'. Coming from a Scouser, that was praise indeed. As was the acknowledgement from Peter Robinson that Paisley loved not only Liverpool FC but the city of Liverpool – 'he was very proud of it, even though he was a Geordie'.

One sports columnist, describing football management as 'the most precarious of professions', wrote that the public perception of a manager 'was a man in a stetson and fur coat whose credibility lasted as long as his fat cigar. In one hand a bottle of Champagne, in the other his morals. It was Bob Paisley who helped give the profession a quiet dignity. The complete antithesis of the self-seeking publicist, he proved over and over again that you did not need to have more front than Harrods to be successful; that decency was no bar to achievement. He gave football managers a code of conduct to live by'.

In his pomp as a player, the Liverpool fans hailed Roger Hunt as Sir Roger. On the day of Paisley's funeral, Hunt recalled Bob Paisley as 'a great man' who had helped not only him, but many other people. The vicar who conducted the service at the church in Woolton spoke of the success Paisley had achieved … 'but success didn't change him'. He remained 'the same, quiet, unassuming Geordie'. That he did. Bob Paisley had worked at the pit, he had been a bricklayer – and, as he once told me, there was a time during his period at Anfield when he felt he would return to being a bricklayer. Instead, he was prevailed upon to stay at Liverpool Football Club where, in his own words, he became 'a part of the furniture'. When he was finally persuaded to become the club's manager, he regarded himself as being 'a buffer' – meaning, when you translated, that he reckoned he would last until Liverpool found someone else.

By the time they did find someone else, 'the buffer' had taken the club to the summit, with silverware galore on the sideboard; and as he prepared to bow out, he was admitting, with that slow smile, that – perhaps to his astonishment – he had actually enjoyed it. Even then, he gave credit to all those who had helped to smooth the path for him. Perhaps above all, Bob Paisley was never a man to boast.

CHAPTER 1

On Your Bike!

WHEN Liverpool signed centre-forward Albert Stubbins from Newcastle United in September, 1946, for a then club-record fee of £13,000, the selling club flashed a message onto the screen at the local cinema asking Stubbins to report at once to St. James's Park. So Albert left the cinema, and when he got to Newcastle United's ground, he discovered that representatives of two clubs – Liverpool *and* Everton – were waiting to talk transfer business with him. So he tossed a coin, and it came down in favour of talking to Liverpool first. By the end of the discussions, manager George Kay had got his man.

There were no messages flashed upon the cinema screen when George Kay signed a young hopeful by the name of Bob Paisley ... although, when he arrived at Lime Street station he was met by one of the club's former players, Andy McGuigan, who by then was on the scouting staff. Paisley, born at Hetton-le-Hole in County Durham, on January 23, 1919, had made his mark as a player with the famed Amateur Cup-fighting club, Bishop Auckland – indeed, when Bishops reached the final in 1939, Liverpool agreed to hold fire on the signing of young Paisley until he had played for Bishops in the big game. They won 3-0, after extra time (shades of what was to happen often enough at Liverpool in the future), and so he landed the first of many mementoes which would long be cherished. Forty years on, and Bob Paisley was celebrating the anniversary of his arrival at Anfield – this time he was manager of Liverpool, and his players (yet again) were collecting medals in the championship ... just as Paisley had done, at the end of season 1946-47.

When he arrived at Lime Street station on May 8, 1939, little did he realise that he would have to wait for six years before he would be able to don a first-team jersey for the first time. As he stepped off the train that day, to be met by Andy McGuigan, he could scarcely have foreseen the events which would take place at Liverpool Football Club, right up to the time of his death. By then, so much had changed in the game he loved.

By his own admission, during season 1995-96, when he was expressing his unhappiness after only four months at Liverpool, Britain's record-priced footballer, Stan Collymore, was earning no less than £12,000 a week. Naturally, Liverpool were unhappy – unhappy that Stan the Man had rushed into print with his views; and after some straight talking Collymore expressed the hope

Boyhood dreams of footballing fame
... the young hopeful, Bob Paisley.

that he would continue to play for the club and that together they would prosper ... as, indeed, they did during the months that followed. By that time, Bob Paisley's days on earth had become numbered, after several years of suffering from the debilitating illness known as Alzheimer's Disease ... perhaps it was as well that he was unable to follow the way the game had gone, with players picking up massive wages and signing-on fees, as they commanded what many people believed to be exhorbitant transfer fees.

Back in 1939, Paisley arrived at Anfield to put pen to paper, and as he signed the forms 'with trembling hand' which made him a Liverpool player, he could reflect upon the fact that after a stint at the pit and a spell as a bricklayer, his new job would be paying him a fiver a week. Oh, yes ... there was a signing-on fee – and that was a tenner. There was no photograph of the event, let alone a Press conference; Liverpool manager George Kay and the young Bob Paisley had agreed everything a couple of weeks previously, up in the North-East. The reason for the delay was the Amateur Cup Final, and Bishops were committed to catching up on a backlog of fixtures which meant that they had to play no fewer than 13 matches in the space of a fortnight. What would the players of today have to say about that?

And what would the players of today say, if the manager suggested that they should cycle 30 miles to the ground, to play in a local cup final? – The answer scarcely bears thinking about … yet that's exactly what Bob Paisley did, during his early days at Liverpool. As a matter of interest, Matt Busby was one of Liverpool's first-teamers around that time, while the great Billy Liddell was in Paisley's age group, along with Ray Lambert, Eddie Spicer and Bill Jones (whose choice for the 1950 F.A. Cup Final, in place of Paisley, was to cause so much argument). Alongside Busby in the first team was Phil Taylor, later to manage the club, and team-mates included Jackie Balmer (a hat-trick hero) and one of several South Africans recruited by Liverpool, Berry 'Nivvy' Nieuwenhuys.

Matt Busby had arrived at Anfield as an £8,000 signing from Manchester City – where, believe it or not, he had once expressed his worry that professional football was 'not my sphere in life'. At that time, he was struggling to make an impact; later, having switched to half-back, he prospered and became one of

Tuning up for the F.A. Cup-tie against Grimsby in 1947 …
Bob Paisley and Jackie Balmer work out in the gym.

Liverpool's finest. And when the war had ended, he was given the chance to join the coaching side, with the hint that the managerial job might well become his. Had he opted to stay, instead of joining Manchester United, one might wonder if Bill Shankly would have ever become the boss at Anfield. Busby's decision to go caused a rift in the lute at Liverpool, to the extent that manager George Kay had to phone him and tell him that the directors had decided they didn't want him to return, to play in an exhibition match. However, the rift was healed with the passing of time, and Busby recalled that it was Liverpool who taught him at least one thing about handling players – they gave one of their playing staff a second benefit, and paid his wages even when he was out of the side.

In those pre-war days, two other players were to graduate to the backroom staff, as Paisley did, later. They were Tom Bush and George Patterson, and even then, it seemed, Liverpool were acquiring a reputation as a club which kept the jobs 'in the family' … just as they did when Paisley succeeded Bill Shankly as manager, and when Joe Fagan followed Paisley, then Kenny Dalglish, Graeme Souness and Roy Evans each got their chance. Oddly enough, Souness was the only one who became team boss after having left Anfield and made his mark as a manager elsewhere. I can recall talking to Bob Paisley shortly before Souness arrived, the second time around … he had been tipped for the job, then it seemed he was set to stay with Glasgow Rangers. When we talked about a possible successor to Kenny Dalglish, whose sudden decision to quit had been such a bombshell, Bob offered the opinion to me that at the end of the day, 'this fellow' would arrive. when I asked him to explain who 'this fellow' might be, he told me: 'Graeme Souness'.

All this, however, was a far cry from the days when young Paisley was striving to succeed as a player. He had signed for the club as a 19-year-old, but he didn't realise that before long there would be a world war – and that the war would lop six years off his life as a professional footballer. By the time the war had intervened, Bob was wondering just where his next stop would be.

The Army had claimed him for its own, and he was stationed at a camp in Cheshire. The place was called Tarporley, and it was about 30 miles from Anfield. In later years, Paisley figured in some notable derby games against Everton, but even so, his first experience of one, at the outset of his career, was memorable, though it was the relatively unimportant final of the Liverpool Senior Cup. While he was in Tarporley, and awaiting a posting overseas, young Paisley was given the word to report to the ground for the derby game, and so he was given a pass by the Army. But … he still had to make his own way to Merseyside. Where there's a will, there's a way … and Bob Paisley wasn't going to pass-up the opportunity of playing against Everton. So he mounted his bike and cycled

Practising his trade as a professional with Liverpool.

there; all 30 miles of it. Recalling this act of devotion which was almost above and beyond the call of duty, Bob told me: 'There was supposed to be a crowd limit – it was 15,000 – but an estimated 30,000 turned up'. Even a Liverpool Senior Cup final had drawing power, when Liverpool and Everton tangled. Sadly for Bob Paisley, it was Everton who took the trophy, by scoring four goals to Liverpool's two.

By the time 1941 had arrived, Bob was on the verge of leaving these shores for a lengthy period; on August Bank holiday of that year, he was setting sail for the Middle East – to be precise, for Egypt – and the journey involved no fewer than 10 weeks at sea. It was no luxury cruise, either, aboard a troopship but, eventually, Gunner Paisley of the Royal Artillery arrived safely. The weeks passed, and Christmas was looming; and so he received his first letter from home. 'It was a note from Liverpool manager George Kay', Bob recalled. 'In it, he told me to report for the first match of the season which was against Preston North End!' That note had followed Gunner Paisley for several thousand miles before it finally caught up with him and, needless to say, he was unavailable for the fixture against North End. He wasn't wasting his time totally, however, because during his stint in the Middle East he came into contact with a jockey by the name of Reg. Stretton and, thereby, he was introduced to the sport of kings. Horses and horse racing became a very real interest – in fact, he rode horses while in Cairo – and at a later stage he met another racing man called Frank Carr. A friendship developed which endured through to the post-war years.

When 'normal service' was resumed, after the war, Frank Carr took up residence as a trainer at Malton, in Yorkshire, and Bob Paisley used to go visiting – and 'mucking out' the stables – during the summer weeks when Soccer wasn't on the agenda. Those were indeed happy days for Bob, and in 1977, when he was waylaid for a This Is Your Life programme, while on the way home (or so he thought) from a game against Queen's Park Rangers in London, Bob had another surprise when he arrived at the studios … Frank Carr had been flown home from Hong Kong for an old comrades' reunion. Bob told me how Carr had fascinated him by the way in which he handled his horses – and, by the same token, the trainer used to tell Paisley that he fascinated him in the way he handled footballers. Bob also told me that during his early days as a manager, he tried to please everyone, but found that it just couldn't be done.

However, those days of management were far distant as the war years took a chunk out of his footballing life. Four years went by, as Paisley served in the desert, and when the shifting sands were left behind and it was on to Italy, the future Liverpool manager finished up entering liberated Rome riding on top of a tank. He was to return in the year 1977, this time to oversee a glorious victory in the final of the European Cup. So, for him, Rome had enduring memories.

His spell in the Army came to an end when he was finally posted back to England and he arrived at Woolwich. Every week, during season 1945-46, he obtained a pass so that he could travel north to play for Liverpool in what were then regional matches. The troops were coming home from theatres of war all around the world, and they demonstrated in no uncertain fashion that they hadn't lost their love for football and their favourite teams. It was in 1946 that Paisley embarked upon the first of four trips to the United States with Liverpool as a player, and their record was impressive, to say the least; they played 34 matches in total, and they won 33 of them, with the single exception being a drawn affair. Once back from that first outing to the States, Bob Paisley settled down to married life with Jessie, whom he had met locally and who remained a constant figure at his side through half a century.

When we talked about football and its impact upon family life, during Bob's years as manager of Liverpool, he said simply: 'I was lucky enough to choose a wife who understood what football meant to me, and what it demanded, in terms of time spent away from home'. He also recalled how, as a five-year-old up in Hetton-le-Hole, he used to see the New Year in by kicking a football around – apparently, this was regarded as a sign that you would become a footballer when you grew up. Certainly, Jessie Paisley appreciated the demands of the job

Across the Atlantic Ocean … and it's Bob Paisley's second trip with Liverpool to the United States. The date: 1948.

Bob did, both as a player and as a manager and – like Nessie Shankly – she was content for the most part to remain in the background, while giving her husband loyal support. I can recall an occasion when Liverpool were once again due to play at Wembley – the place they came to call Anfield South – and on the eve of the final we had gathered at the team's hotel as guests of the club. The players and their manager, of course, were elsewhere, in preparation for the stern business of bringing home a trophy, but the rest of us could enjoy a convivial, social evening and we did. I came down in the lift for dinner with my wife, and there were two more people in the lift – one of them was Jessie Paisley. She had a flower in her lapel; otherwise, she was quietly dressed and, while she smiled at you, if you hadn't realised who she was you could have mistaken her for just another, anonymous guest in the hotel, instead of the wife of one of football's most famous figures. Like her husband, she preferred the quiet life to the glitzy occasion.

If Bob Paisley won so much praise for his achievements as a manager, he was highly regarded for his ability as a footballer – a tenacious wing-half, he showed courage (not least when it came to overcoming injuries) and loyalty (when it came to putting the team before himself). In 1947, for example, when Liverpool met Burnley in the semi-finals of the F.A. Cup, his direct opponent was Billy

Morris, of whom it was recorded: 'A forward like that needs an escort of two men and a terrier'. And then came this tribute to the Liverpool wing-half: 'Paisley played like two men and a terrier'. Another description of Paisley the player: 'He stands five feet seven inches tall, is 11 stone of muscle, and has a never-say-die spirit'. In the fifth round of the F.A. Cup in 1947, when Liverpool knocked out the holders, Derby County, 'Paisley blotted out Carter (the legendary Raich Carter), and this was the primary reason County were ousted from the Cup'.

On one notable occasion, there was a battle royal between Paisley and the wizard of dribble, Stanley Matthews, who was then wearing the tangerine shirt of Blackpool. A contemporary report ran like this: 'Paisley went in, was beaten, then had the temerity to go back for more. The result was that Matthews, who had left him yards behind, suddenly found the second tackle the lethal one. Matthews mesmerised Lambert, but he did no such thing to Paisley'. There was also a reference to Phil Taylor, Bill Jones and Bob Paisley as 'one of the finest half-back lines in the country', with this description of Paisley: 'Little height, two stout limbs, a heart of gold and a tackle that is riotous. He has become the complete half-back, with tenacity written all over his face. His powerful throw-ins could be worth a lot of goals. Opposition forwards are never given a moment's

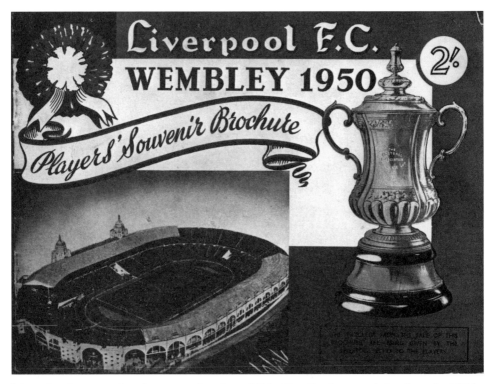

Memories, happy and unhappy … the players' F.A. Cup-final souvenir brochure in 1950 – when Bob Paisley was axed from the Wembley side, on a split vote by the directors.

peace when Bob is around – he doesn't know the word "defeat". Not until the final whistle are opposing forwards free from Paisley's attentions'. Liverpool, remember, during the days when Shankly was their manager, often won a match in the final minutes … and that, surely, was one of the secrets of their success – that they never, ever gave up until the final whistle had gone.

Courage in adversity? – This was a report upon the incident when Paisley the player went down as if pole-axed: 'When they elect the Footballer of the Year at the end of the season, they will doubtless choose some much-publicised figure, glamorous for a succession of caps and other football brilliance which seems to count for all today. It will surprise me if they so much as mention the name of Robert Paisley; but if they did, it would be the finest tribute to the vast mass of good club players. For Paisley, in a football sense, gives his all till it hurts. Even then, he refuses to lie down and be treated as casualties usually are. Struck on the side of the head and concussed by a tremendous shot by Dodgin early in the match at Newcastle, Paisley was knocked unconscious, but resumed at outside-left. Ten minutes before the interval he was so shaky, trainer Albert Shelley had to carry him off.

'During the interval, the unusual method of walking him up and down outside the main grandstand was used, in the hope that he would come to. Nine minutes after the match restarted, Paisley trotted on again, to do useful work at outside-

Bob Paisley in Action for Liverpool against Aston Villa

left before trying to head a goal off a Liddell centre and falling unconscious for a second time'.

Not surprisingly, they carried Bob Paisley from the field of play once more, and this time they took him to hospital so that he could be X-rayed. They kept him in the hospital, too. And years later, when Bob discussed the incident with me, he told me: 'I remembered nothing after the first 10 minutes. When I came to, I was dressed – and my father, who had been at the match, was angry with me for going on a second time and for daring to head the ball again. It was hard work convincing him that I didn't even remember coming back, much less trying to score!'

Injury cost Bob Paisley a place in the 1950 F.A. Cup Final, in a manner of speaking, and his Dad was an angry man on that occasion, as well ... so angry, indeed, that he refused to attend the final. But his son was there, trying to hide his deep disappointment and displaying the kind of loyalty to Liverpool Football Club which was the hallmark of his service through half a century and more. There was indeed a touch of irony about Liverpool's victory over Grimsby Town in the fourth round of the competition in 1950, because both Paisley and Bill Jones, the man who won the vote over him, were singled out for praise. 'Jones and Paisley were superb ... Paisley was a dour tackler, giving an indefatigable display and contributing some dazzling solo runs. One, during which he beat three men by the adroitness of his heading, was masterly'. Come the final, and Liverpool lived to rue the moment the decision was taken to axe Paisley from their Wembley line-up.

CHAPTER 2

Sweating it Out

SOME people have suffered the bitter-sweet experience of flirting with relegation while, at the same time, heading towards Wembley. It happened to Matt Busby when he was manager of Manchester United, in season 1962-63. United were seemingly threatened with the drop, and Busby – mulling over the best way to get his team out of trouble – was given a vote of confidence by his chairman, Harold Hardman. By the end of the season the former Liverpool star had ensured a narrow escape from relegation, and was celebrating F.A. Cup success at Leicester City's expense.

Bob Paisley and his Liverpool team-mates kicked off season 1946-47 with high hopes – as usual. But in fairly quick time they appeared to be very live candidates for relegation, even though Liverpool had in their ranks some fine players. Apart from Paisley, they had Welsh-internationals Ray Lambert and Cyril Sidlow, marksman Jackie Balmer, the cultured Phil Taylor, Bill Jones and Laurie Hughes (both of whom were to gain representative honours), Cyril Done, Billy Liddell and another Scot by the name of Jim Harley, who possessed a real turn of pace – indeed, he was a Powderhall-sprint handicap winner … and that cost him a tenner because he missed training.

Taylor, later to manage Liverpool, might well have carved out a career in another sport – cricket – and he was certainly fancied by Gloucestershire; but football won the vote, and he signed for Liverpool from Bristol Rovers, his local club. Many years later, he was still in touch with Anfield affairs, and joining up with Bob Paisley and Billy Liddell for a reunion and a talk about old times. Originally an inside-forward – he kicked off with Liverpool by scoring a goal at Derby – he switched with great success to wing-half.

Taylor had a real touch of class about him, and he emerged as a successor to Matt Busby as he captained the side and went on to claim an England place. He totalled close on 350 appearances for Liverpool, led the team out for the 1950 F.A. Cup final at Wembley, and played his final game during the relegation season of 1953-54, before joining the backroom staff, as Bob Paisley did. If Taylor oozed class, so did another player who skippered Liverpool – Willie Fagan, recruited from Preston North End. He could control the ball in an instant, beat his man in George Best style, with a swivel of the hips, and when he shot for

Liverpool's F.A. Cup semi-final team of 1947 …

Back row (left to right): Manager George Kay, Jim Harley, Phil Taylor, Ray Lambert, Cyril Sidlow, Bob Paisley, Bill Jones, Billy Liddell, Albert Shelley (trainer).

Front row: Willie Fagan, Jackie Balmer, Bill McConnell (chairman), Albert Stubbins, Cyril Done.

goal, he packed a powerful punch in his boots. Just like Jackie Balmer, one of the handful of players who crossed the park from Everton to Anfield.

There were other personalities in the side – like Balmer, Done was a local lad, while goalkeeper Sidlow had been spotted and signed for Wolves by the man who became famous for getting players super-fit by what became known as the 'monkey-gland' treatment. Major Frank Buckley became a household name for his pioneering style of treatment for footballers around that time. As for Sidlow, he was signed by Liverpool in time to play for them in the F.A. Cup semi-final against Burnley, and he cost the club what would now be a derisory £4,000 – compare this to the cash laid out for David James. Sidlow gained fame not only because he was an accomplished 'keeper - he had won 11 Welsh caps during wartime – but because he was one of the first to use the long throw to an outfield player, rather than boot the ball almost out of sight. He was capped seven times while with Liverpool, and played 165 games for the club.

Another notable signing was Albert Stubbins, who cost a club-record fee of £13,000, and he became a real favourite with the Anfield faithful … as, of course, did a player who cost the club nothing. His name was Billy Liddell. Like Stubbins, he soon showed that he knew how to find the net. Stubbins had already achieved near-immortality with Newcastle United, for whom he totalled 244 goals, and he was to tack on 83 more goals during his 180 appearances for Liverpool, who had snatched him from under the noses of Everton. Albert himself told me the story of the fateful day when he had 'gone to the pictures' and seen his name flashed on the screen as the message came for him to report back to St. James's Park.

When he arrived, it was to find that Liverpool manager George Kay and Everton manager Theo. Kelly were awaiting his pleasure, and after a coin had been tossed it was Liverpool who won the day. Albert told me: 'Everton were very disappointed at missing out, but they took it very sportingly, and wished me all the best with Liverpool'. In quick time, Stubbins was knocking in the goals and Liverpool were heading for a League-title trophy. Albert scored on his debut, hit a hat-trick in a sixth-round F.A. Cup-tie against Birmingham – one of his goals became known as 'the goal in the snow' as he flung himself at the ball and headed it home. The cross had been provided by Billy Liddell.

This young Scot had arrived at Anfield from Lochgelly, and Matt Busby told me how he played a part initially in Billy landing at Anfield. Quiet and modest, just like Bob Paisley, Billy held down a part-time job, and he and I used to meet now and then after he had finished training, and we would go and have a cup of coffee at the old Kardomah cafe. He stayed at Anfield for more than 15 years, totalled 537 appearances and scored 229 goals; and not for nothing was he known as the Flying Scot, while some fans called their team Liddellpool. Like Paisley, he became a legend in his own lifetime, and this long-term friend of Bob's was one of the mourners at his funeral.

Jackie Balmer achieved fame by virtue of having scored hat-tricks in three consecutive matches during that championship season of 1946-47, and he thus became the first footballer to achieve such a feat in the League. He notched a hat-trick against Portsmouth, at Anfield; went one better as he scored four goals away against Derby County; then returned home to rattle in another trio of goals against Arsenal. Remarkably, this meant that Balmer had not only totalled 10 goals in three successive outings ... he had done so without a single other Liverpool player having found the net. He totalled more than 110 goals in his 313 appearances for Liverpool, and there was no doubt that Everton were made to rue the day they allowed him to cross Stanley Park. Other clubs were made to rue the day they came up against Liverpool during that championship season, as well ... though it was touch and go at the finish, because there was a nail-biting climax to the campaign.

Under the management of Bill Shankly, Bob Paisley, Joe Fagan and Kenny

Dalglish, Liverpool Football Club has known some great days, enjoyed some tremendous triumphs – yet season 1946-47 became one of the most glorious chapters in the club's history as the team powered its way forward, both in the League and on the F.A. Cup front. In the League, Liverpool had been very close to the bottom rung of the table, and the know-alls were starting to predict that relegation was very much on the cards; then, the team began to click and the result was a run of a dozen matches without one defeat. Suddenly, instead of relegation the talk was of championship medals. As for the F.A. Cup, Liverpool went through the third, fourth, fifth and sixth rounds to come up against Burnley in the semi-finals – and it took a replay before the Turf Moor club claimed a place at Wembley.

So it was back to the League-title chase, and with seven matches remaining, Liverpool were very definitely second favourites to carry off the trophy. They had to admit that Wolves appeared to have it wrapped up … the men from Molineux were no fewer than nine points clear; and what was more, five of Liverpool's last seven games were away from home. It was then that Liverpool demonstrated what they have demonstrated so often since – that a game is never lost until the final whistle has gone, and that you cannot bank upon a trophy until it is safely on the sideboard. Liverpool pegged away to such good effect that they collected 13 out of 14 points, while Wolves managed just one point out of the 14 for which they were playing. So Wolves finished in third place – shades of Manchester United during the 1980's, when they reeled off 10 straight wins at the start, yet ended up in fourth spot while Liverpool took the title.

Even so, in season 1946-47, Liverpool were made to sweat it out right to the last gasp, because although Wolves faltered and fell at the final hurdle, another club – Stoke City – could still spoil the Anfield championship celebrations. Stoke had to go to Bramall Lane, and if they managed to beat Sheffield United there they could pip Liverpool for the title.

All in all, it turned out to be an extraordinary season, not least because the weather played a part. This meant that the campaign carried on beyond its scheduled finishing date … while Liverpool went to Molineux for their final League match, on the last day of May, the decisive encounter did not take place until a couple of weeks after that. And this was the situation, as Liverpool travelled to the Midlands for their duel with Wolves (whose captain, Stan Cullis, was about to hang up his playing boots and become the club's assistant manager)… At the top, it was Manchester United, leading on goal average and with 56 points in the bag – but also having played their final game; right behind were Wolves, also on 56 points, and with their date against Liverpool giving them the chance to overhaul United; and right behind them were Liverpool, just a point adrift and needing to win at Molineux, if they were to have a chance of landing the championship. All of which left Stoke City as the club which would come surging through to pip the lot of them – providing that they could get the better of Sheffield United at Bramall Lane. Victory there would enable Stoke to claim the title on goal average. So the stage was set for a battle royal between Wolves and Liverpool – and the folk who saw the match were not to be disappointed ... especially those who had travelled from Merseyside!

After the terrible weather which had caused the season to be extended, it was an evening for the fans to bask in a more balmy atmosphere – indeed, many of them went shirt-sleeved to Molineux – although the temperature became even hotter as the tension rose. It was a goal from Balmer which put Liverpool in the driving seat, just inside half an hour – he rounded off a four-man move which had involved Spicer, Liddell and Priday. With half-time looming, Liverpool fans went delirious with delight as Stubbins lashed in a 20-yard rocket to beat Bert Williams in the Wolves goal. Wolves fought back in the second half, and they managed a goal through Dunn, but they couldn't deny Liverpool their victory, even though the men from Anfield were finding it hard going, with Hughes and Liddell hobbling. But the 50,000 spectators left Molineux knowing that Liverpool's 2-1 victory had killed off Wolves and Manchester United ... now it was up to Stoke, who were due to play at Bramall Lane on June 14. Meanwhile, Liverpool's players concentrated on beating Everton in the final of the Liverpool Senior Cup ... then they sweated it out before learning that Stoke had lost, 2-1.

Taken all round, it was a season of success for Liverpool, because apart from the First Division championship, they collected the Liverpool Senior Cup, the Lancashire Senior Cup and the Lancashire County Combination Championship Cup. In later years (1975-76, to be exact), when Bob Paisley was Liverpool's manager, Wolves were to suffer again, this time as Liverpool went to Molineux, trailed to a Steve Kindon goal – then struck back to emerge not only as the winners, but as the First Division champions.

Bob Paisley's career lasted through nine post-war seasons, and during that time he totalled close on 280 first-team appearances and scored 13 goals. One of those goals turned out to be lucky for Liverpool, because it put them on the road to Wembley ... but the omens were not so good for the man who scored it. Yet before that day in 1950, Paisley and his team-mates were to endure the ups and downs of football, just as they had savoured the delights of taking the title. By season 1949-50, Paisley had clocked up a century of first-team outings, and as Liverpool made progress in the F.A. Cup, he found himself in and out of the side.

He was as tough as teak, as was demonstrated when he was carried off twice during that match at Newcastle, and while he made light of knocks there were one or two occasions when he came off worst – for example, in a match at

Blackpool's Bloomfield Road ground. Bob and a team-mate went up together for the ball – and as they both tried to head it clear, they collided. Paisley's head was split open, his team-mate broke his nose in no fewer than six places. There was also a match against Charlton Athletic when Paisley went up to head away a corner and he was caught by the knee of Charlton's Chris Duffy (their match-winner in the 1947 F.A. Cup final against Burnley, who had knocked Liverpool off the Wembley trail at the semi-final stage). Duffy's knee broke four of Paisley's ribs.

Goals in the F.A. Cup are usually to be savoured by the player who scores them, especially if that player isn't noted for being a marksman – and Bob Paisley's record in that respect was not calculated to make headlines ... except on one occasion. True, he struck a last-minute equaliser in a tie against Nottingham Forest (Liverpool won the replay, 4-1) and the winner in a 2-1 success against Wolves ... that match was watched by a record Anfield crowd of more than 61,000. But it was the F.A. Cup campaign in season 1949-50 which was memorable.

Paisley had suffered an injury while playing against Blackburn Rovers at Ewood Park, but managed to make the replay – ironically, he then replaced Bill Jones, who had become a casualty (and who was to replace Paisley on the big day at Wembley). Liverpool went on to win the replay, and they defeated Grimsby Town, Derby County and Birmingham City. Then came the semi-final against Everton, and on this occasion Paisley emerged as a headliner, the man whose goal had helped to take Liverpool through to the final. The match was played at Manchester City's Maine Road ground, and it ended in general agreement that this had been the greatest derby game of all time ... although in later years, when Kenny Dalglish was Liverpool's manager, the 4-4 draw at Goodison Park was made even more sensational with the bombshell news next day that Dalglish had quit his job.

Back to the 1950 semi-final against Everton, however, and as the Liverpool fans in the crowd roared encouragement, Jimmy Payne took the ball down the right-hand side of the field, then sent over a cross. Everton 'keeper George Burnett came off his line and went up to punch the ball clear – and, as it dropped, it fell to Bob Paisley. Immediately, he lobbed the ball back towards Burnett's goal, and as it looped through the air, Billy Liddell went up to challenge the 'keeper and an Everton defender, while two more Everton players – Moore and Hedley – stood guard on the goal-line. But nobody managed to get even a touch to the ball; it simply dipped and went over the line and into the net.

When Bob Paisley recalled this golden moment, he told me something else – that manager George Kay had given him some sharp advice about a week before the semi-final. It was to the effect that he should forget about going in search of a goal and concentrate instead upon his defensive duties. But there was Paisley, not far out from goal, when Burnett punched it clear. Bob told me: 'When the ball fell to me, instinctively I was going to try for a shot. Then the manager's warning flashed across my mind – so I just lobbed the ball forward, hoping a team-mate would apply the finishing touch'. Billy Liddell was Liverpool's other marksman, and so Wembley beckoned for him and his team-mates ... but not, unhappily, for Paisley. He recalled: 'I had taken a knock, and so I missed a League match, in order to make sure that I had recovered in time for the final. It was the worst thing I could have done'.

Sure enough, Paisley had recovered in time for the final ... only to learn that there would be no place for him in the Liverpool line-up at Wembley. He didn't even have the consolation of thinking that he might be called up at some stage of the game, either, because in those days there was no such thing as substitutes. And what made things all the worse for him was the fact that he learned of his omission when he picked up the evening paper and read that the vote had gone against him and in favour of Bill Jones.

In those days, the directors decided upon the team; indeed, Bill Shankly became the first Liverpool manager to have sole control over picking the side. So, no matter what George Kay, the team boss in 1950, may have thought, the final decision rested with the members of the board – it seemed that they had been split almost down the middle, because four of them were in favour of Paisley, with five coming down on the side of Jones. To say that Paisley was disappointed is an understatement; indeed, he told me: 'I came very, very close to asking Liverpool for a transfer at that time; and my father was so incensed about my being left out that he refused to go to the game'. Paisley himself swallowed the bitter pill of disappointment, however, and took his place on the bench as an onlooker.

It was a match which Arsenal won 2-0, and Bob recalled: 'For me, it was ironic that I sat there and watched Jimmy Logie laying on both goals for Reg. Lewis, because Logie was the man I would have been marking – and twice that season I'd been his marker in League matches, coming out on top each time, as Liverpool won. Another irony about the situation was that Bill Jones, who took my place at left-half, was really a centre-half – a week later, he was picked for an England tour. True, Bill had played in several positions for the club, but when he was chosen for an international tour, it was at centre-half'. The one consolation for Bob Paisley was that a special medal was struck for him, to go with his Amateur Cup-winner's medal. But it didn't make up for the heartache of that Wembley day in 1950. And there was plenty of comment about the directors' decision to omit him from the team. One headline declared that PAISLEY PUT EVERTON OUT OF THE CUP – AND HE MAY NOT BE THERE AT WEMBLEY. Paisley was also rated as 'Sportsman of the Year'.

One commentator summed up: 'My verdict is that the Anfield bosses made perhaps the biggest blunder in post-war Soccer history when they dropped Paisley and Balmer… The dropping of Paisley was a tragic error. Paisley, with the streak of attacking thrust which won Liverpool their Wembley passport, might have matched Arsenal's Forbes in essential aggressiveness. Liverpool's attack always played too far back. The Liverpool chiefs who chose the team chose defeat. Meantime Paisley sat, a forlorn-looking figure on a touchline bench, his feet twitching and itching to kick the ball'. And the quote from Paisley himself which earned that 'Sportsman-of-the-Year' tag: 'I'm deeply disappointed, but Cup-final eve is no time to worry your manager and team-mates with private matters. I only hope my club wins without me'. Now … would you expect any of today's highly-paid stars to express similar sentiments, should they be axed from an F.A. Cup-final side? – Hardly…

If Paisley was deeply disappointed, Liverpool suffered twice over, because up to a week before the final they had been in with a shout for the League title; but when Portsmouth upset that apple-cart, the championship became no more than a mirage, and the final turned out to be the last straw for manager George Kay. He had worked hard and long in the cause of the Anfield club, and he had seen two prizes snatched from Liverpool's grasp. The strain of it all had taken its toll, and not long after the Wembley debacle he tendered his resignation. It was the start of a period of hope and despair for Liverpool and their faithful supporters, as the club see-sawed, finally suffered relegation, and then had to endure a series of near-misses before the dawn finally broke once more.

In March, 1951, Liverpool had a new manager. His name was Don Welsh, and he had once scored six goals for them in a match against Southport, when he figured as a guest player during the war years. Welsh had had a distinguished career as a player – his name was synonymous with Charlton Athletic – and he had endeared himself to the Anfield faithful when he struck a hat-trick in each half as Liverpool hammered Southport 12-1. While with Charlton, he had helped the London club rise from the Third Division (South) to become First Division runners-up – all this in the space of three seasons. He was a big man, and he had presence; Liverpool also hoped he had what it took to steer them to further success. In the event, Welsh reigned at Anfield from 1951 to 1956, and he splashed what, at the time, were substantial transfer fees on new faces.

Welsh went to Wolves and paid £12,000 for Sammy Smyth, and he raided the transfer market again, spending more than £50,000 in total; he also blooded players such as Ronnie Moran, Louis Bimpson and Alan A'Court; but though the defence had a firm enough look about it, the Liverpool attack was lacking in menace. This was a side which was growing old, and it showed in the results – although during the season after the 1950 F.A. Cup final Bob Paisley played in

41 matches, to become the man with the highest number of appearances. In season 1951-52, he also made it into the England B squad which went on tour to Holland. That season, in fact, was virtually Paisley's final fling as a player, and the club had a very close shave as it battled to stave off relegation.

When Liverpool came up against Chelsea, victory was imperative ... and the Anfield Reds managed it, scoring twice without reply. So they earned a reprieve – but it was short-lived, for it lasted only a season. By the half-way stage in the next campaign, Liverpool had picked up 19 points, although the older players were finding themselves surplus to first-team requirement. The last 21 games saw Liverpool collecting no more than nine points, and this made relegation a certainty. Paisley was to say later: 'I'm sure relegation could have been avoided – and eight years in the Second Division – if we had started rebuilding a little earlier'. When it had become apparent that there was no escaping the drop, he and a few more of the old brigade were recalled into the side, but as Liverpool went down, Paisley, Jones, Taylor and Spicer all hung up their boots.

By that time, Paisley was taking an interest in the backroom science of physiotherapy – he took a correspondence course, and backed this up by visiting hospitals to learn how equipment was used to enable patients to regain full fitness. It was a man from the opposition camp at Everton – John Moores – who arranged for Bob to see for himself on those hospital trips, while Liverpool director T.V. Williams played a key role in persuading the former player to become a trainer. Bob told me: 'There was a time when it seemed I might be going back to brick-laying – that was what was in my mind. I wonder how things would have turned out then – for Liverpool, was well as for me?'

While Don Welsh did his utmost to achieve promotion for the club, he also introduced players such as Jimmy Melia – who figured prominently in the Shankly era when promotion was finally achieved – but although Liverpool managed to finish in third place at the end of season 1955-56, it wasn't good enough to see them up, and Welsh went through the exit door. As for Paisley, he found himself calling his former team-mate, Phil Taylor, 'the boss'; and Bob himself was not doing so badly as a backroom man. His first season in charge of the reserve team ended with a finishing place of sixth in the Central League; the second time out, Liverpool's reserves claimed the runners-up spot; and at the end of the third term they collected the Central League championship trophy ... which meant that Bob Paisley, even so early in his career behind the scenes, had helped to make a bit of club history, since that was the first time Liverpool had won this particular trophy.

Phil Taylor went so close to doing the business. He strengthened the first team by signing goalkeeper Tommy Younger from Hibernian, and the Scotland international became a firm favourite with the fans. 'Big Tam' was a genial character and a fine 'keeper – in his three seasons at Anfield he totalled 127 appearances, missing only half a dozen League games. Taylor also recruited Johnny Wheeler from Bolton, Tony McNamara and Jimmy Harrower – like Younger, a Scot. And promotion was tantalisingly close … towards the end of Taylor's first term in charge, Liverpool finished with a real flourish as they won seven and drew two of their last 10 games – but they still had to settle for third place. By then, A'Court was claiming representative honours, as was Ronnie Moran, when he was called up to play for the Football League, and when season 1957-58 came around, there was plenty of cause for optimism. Once more, however, Liverpool faltered, as they finished fourth and missed the promotion boat by a couple of points. And there was a poor start to the following season, which was notable for three things … Billy Liddell was dropped for the first time, Liverpool were knocked out of the F.A. Cup by non-league Worcester City … and, once again they could do no better than finish fourth. On November 17, 1959, Phil Taylor called it quits, saying: 'I'm tired. The strain of trying to win promotion has proved too much'.

So once again Liverpool were looking for a new manager, and this time when they made their choice, they didn't keep the job 'in the family' – they went to Huddersfield Town for a Scot who called a spade a spade, and who in his time as a player had won international honours and medals. His name was Bill Shankly, and he had served his managerial apprenticeship at Soccer outposts such as Grimsby Town, Carlisle United and Workington, before moving to Huddersfield as the No. 2 to another famous name, Andy Beattie. When Beattie came to the end of his managerial stint at Huddersfield, Shankly stepped into the job. But the call came for him to take his chance with Liverpool, and on December 1, 1959, he was officially named as 'the boss'. It was an appointment which was to change not only the fortunes of the Anfield club, but the life of one Robert Paisley. He was already there, but at that moment in time he had no vision of the fame which awaited him. As ever, all he looked for was to carry on working as well as he knew how in the service of the club which had become his life.

CHAPTER 3

Softly, Softly …

NESSIE SHANKLY reflected upon the two men she had known so well through many years – her husband, Bill, and the stocky Geordie who had been his loyal partner, Bob Paisley. 'The Terrible Twins', as she termed this pair of footballing characters. Now both of them are dead; yet so many memories remained. And Nessie, quietly spoken, confirmed something which I had long suspected, yet had failed to elicit from all my conversations with Bob. That there were times when Bill's right-hand man had, in effect, acted as a restraining influence upon Liverpool's manager.

I did once suggest to Bob that I felt he had occasionally steered Bill away from doing something or saying something he might later regret, or that he might now and again have planted an idea in Bill's mind. Bob just smiled, and said nothing. He didn't give much away … as Nessie Shankly said: 'He always thought before he spoke'. That wasn't always the case with Bill – Nessie, reflecting upon his days on this earth, recalled that there were times when he would admit: 'I shouldn't have said that'. Bob Paisley admitted that 'If I can go down the street and not be recognised, I'm delighted'. It wasn't quite so with Bill … as Bob said, with a smile, he had steel tips on his shoes and you could hear him coming. Well, I never saw steel tips on Bill's shoes, but I know what Bob meant.

Nessie reflected: 'I think that, in a way, Bill needed Bob. I think he calmed him down a bit. Sometimes Bill would flare up. Bob would bring him down to earth'. Bob himself never forgot a piece of advice which his old headmaster had once given him. 'He told me that if you had something to say to someone, then you should speak softly … that way, they would listen. And that's the approach I tried to take'.

Shankly on the balcony, addressing the massed ranks of the Liverpool faithful after yet another success for the Anfield club: 'It's you who we play for … you're the ones who pay our wages'. Bill almost made statements such as this seem like a prediction of the Second Coming. Bill could harangue the fans and his words would be greeted with delight by the folk who came close to adoring him. He could also be brusque and leave a listener somewhat disconcerted – that happened more than once, with me. For example, after Liverpool had suffered a mauling at the hands of Ajax, in a European match in Holland, we were in his office at Anfield discussing the return game and, clearly, Liverpool had it all to do.

If you knew Shankly, you took a leaf from Bob Paisley's book – you thought before you spoke; otherwise, you risked his wrath or some cutting reply. On this occasion, I considered what to say, and then I ventured the opinion that the return game would prove a stern test for Liverpool. Since they were already 5-1 down, I didn't see how Bill Shankly could offer me any argument. But I was taken aback when he looked straight at me, then declared forcefully: 'Ajax? – They're just a bunch of bluidy peasants!' Plainly, there was no more to be said.

On another occasion, when I had written an article for a magazine detailing what Liverpool had achieved in the way of trophies, Bill and I met at Prenton Park, where Tranmere Rovers were playing that evening. Bill button-holed me and told me: 'That was a guid piece ye did, Stan…' Coming from him, this as praise indeed, and I almost glowed as I listened to his words. Then, of course, came the put down, as he added the sting in the tail. 'But ye forgot one thing … ye didna' mention that we won the Charity Shield!' Consider yourself told off … just as a scribe was when, after a League match at Anfield one Saturday afternoon, we awaited Bill's pleasure. As usual, he walked down the corridor from the players' dressing-room and addressed us. 'Hello, boys' – that was the normal greeting. Then a few seconds would pass by as Bill looked down at his polished black shoes, and finally someone would be brave enough to set the ball rolling with a comment or question concerning the afternoon's proceedings. On this occasion, Liverpool had suffered a reverse – and that didn't happen often at Anfield. So, of course, the first comment or question could be tricky, to say the least.

Naturally, the Merseyside-based reporters were there, and so were some from further afield. It was one of the latter who waded straight in with the comment – not a question, but a statement – that 'Liverpool didn't play very well today, Bill'. Shankly continued to look down at his shoes for a few more seconds, while those of us who knew him winced inwardly at the temerity of the reporter who had mad the remark. Then Liverpool's manager looked up, stared straight through the offending reporter, and observed, unblinkingly: 'Don't lean on that wall – it's just been painted!' Well, there's no answer to that – and there wasn't.

It was typical of Shankly that on his arrival he made it clear to his backroom staff, as Bob Paisley told me, that there must be no cliques. All for one, and one for all was the motto; and that was how it was. At the very outset, Shankly saw the team he was leaving at Huddersfield defeat the team he was inheriting at Liverpool, and he declared that 'at least Liverpool did fight'. His first match in charge at Anfield ended with Liverpool conceding four goals against Cardiff City, and afterwards Bill was said to have walked into the boardroom and defiantly assured his directors: 'Gentlemen, we will win a match at Anfield this season!'

Liverpool, in fact, were to lose very few matches on home ground during Shankly's tenure of office.

When Nessie Shankly spoke about Bill and his admission that 'I shouldn't have said that', it reminded me of another experience I had with Liverpool's manager, at a time when I had just resigned my job at the local evening paper, where I had been in charge of the sports department. Liverpool were flying off on another European safari, and this would be my final trip with them on behalf of the paper. We were all meeting up at Speke airport, and as I walked in through one door, Bill walked in through another, so that we were heading towards each other. Players and Press were there, standing around and chatting. Suddenly, that rasping voice of Bill's cut into all the chatter as he addressed me – and what he said ended the all-round babble of conversation. 'I hear ye're leaving that paper, Stan', was Bill's opening remark. And when I acknowledged that this was true, he barked: 'Well, ye're no' a bad judge!' The only thing I could think of was to tell him: 'Well, you said that, Bill, not me!'

Early on in Shankly's career as Liverpool manager, after the team had lost a match, Bill would have no truck with those who tried to sympathise with him. 'Save your sympathy… I can look after myself, and I can look after my team!' And, of course, he proved that to the hilt as Liverpool achieved so many honours at home and abroad during his term as the boss. Carlisle, Grimsby, Workington and Huddersfield had all been stepping-stones along the way to managerial greatness, and while he discarded more than a score of players as he rebuilt, he didn't muck about with the backroom staff. There were a few near-misses before promotion was gained, but once Liverpool were back in the First Division, it was almost a case of the sky's the limit.

Yet early on, Shankly was something of a mystery man to his backroom team. After a Saturday match at Anfield, he would pick up a football and track suit and take his leave, because he was then still living in Yorkshire. Bob Paisley recalled: 'We used to wonder what Bill was doing, when we saw him going off like that. Eventually, we did manage to solve the mystery – we discovered that Bill was taking the ball and the tracksuit because every Sunday morning he was going for a kickabout with the locals over there'.

Bill Shankly was Bill Shankly, just as Bob Paisley was Bob Paisley, and together they made a formidable team. Bob summed up his own philosophy when he said: 'You have to be yourself. If you stray from that line, there's nothing for you; at the end of the day, if it's not good enough, then you have to accept that'. When he looked at you, his eyes sometimes appeared to be hooded by lids that almost closed, and he was described as 'a wily old fox with a complete understanding of the game'. Indeed, it was while I was working at the local evening paper at Liverpool that I came to the conclusion that this man, who seemed to live in the shadow of Bill Shankly, had seen so much of the way things were run at Liverpool that he must have a decent story to tell; if he could be persuaded to tell it. I had no intention of asking Bob to dish the dirt; I simply felt that there must be a lot of good stories he could relate, without giving anyone offence. And when he was approached, my assumption turned out to be correct.

Shankly's right-hand man had never been one to thrust himself into the limelight, but he was possessed of a unique knowledge about what went on behind the scenes at Anfield, and what he had to say made extremely interesting reading – even if you had to listen hard, at times, to decipher what he was saying in that Geordie accent of his. Naturally, I wondered how much Bob Paisley would want, when it came to the cash side of the equation – you could hardly ask him to do something for nothing. In the event, he didn't ask for a penny, but I felt that we must pay him something – and he received the munificent amount of £80 for his time and trouble. I doubt if any of today's footballers would even consider telling you what time it was, for such a piffling sum.

I first met Bill Shankly during his days at Huddersfield, and we talked then in what seemed to be a dungeon-like shed under the maind stand – I think it was painted dark green. Our paths continued to cross once he had gone to Liverpool, and at the start of the 1970's I got the job of editing the club's match-day programme, which meant doing all the writing – including Bill's programme notes. So I used to ring him at home, ask him if there was anything in particular he wanted to say, and then we would get down to the details. Once I had written the stuff, I would send Bill a copy, then check with him that he was happy about it. I cannot recall him ever telling me to alter anything, so he must have been satisfied – except on one occasion, when the piece I had done seemed such a good one that it was worthy of a wider audience than the fans who bought the programme on a Saturday afternoon.

I spoke to the editor of a national magazine which specialised in football matters, and he was enthusiastic about the piece – even though I stressed that nothing could be done until I'd spoken to Bill and the piece had appeared in the programme. The editor was happy enough to go along with that – but Shanks wasn't. I had barely started to tell him what I had in mind before he was jumping down my throat and telling me: 'That piece is for the programme – and nowhere else!' And that was how it was.

Not until many years later did I learn that before I had even been invited to take on the job of editing Liverpool's programme, their manager had been asked if he felt he could work with me. When I found out that he had given his assent, I felt rather gratified, because it seemed to signify that he felt he could trust me. Whether or not he still felt this, after our little altercation about the programme piece I had wanted to use elsewhere, I wouldn't know. I do know that he had a way of his own – and his way certainly suited the Liverpool fans. 'He and the Kop were made for each other', said Paisley. 'I knew the Kop from my playing days, and I knew what sort of a man and a player they appreciated'. They appreciated Bob Paisley, too.

As Shankly rebuilt the Liverpool team, he went 'straight down the middle', with Tommy Lawrence in goal, Ron Yeats at centre-half, and Ian St. John up front. Shankly was to say that on his arrival, 'I was disappointed with many things, but my training and coaching staff never gave me a moment's anxiety. I have a real team behind the team'. But – starting with a defeat at Anfield – Liverpool garnered only one point from their first three matches in the top flight, and the 50,000 fans who had witnessed Blackpool beat them on their own ground went home pondering on the team's future. The backroom team deliberated on the need for a wing-half, and one morning after he had gone down to Anfield expecting to supervise a training session, Paisley was despatched on another mission. In later years, he was to vet both Kevin Keegan and Steve Heighway for Shankly; this time, his manager had told him: 'Get yourself up tae Glasgae ...' The player under the microscope was called Willie Stevenson, and he was languishing in Rangers' reserve side. Paisley checked him out, and there were one or two more scouting trips to watch Stevenson – then he arrived at Anfield as a £27,000 fee changed hands.

Paisley told me, too, about a player who was with Shankly's old club, Preston North End ... Peter Thompson. 'He had always been a thorn in our side when the teams met, and once we landed him, Bill Shankly reckoned he was the final piece in the jigsaw puzzle'. That false start in August, 1963 – defeats at home by Nottingham Forest, Blackpool and West Ham – was followed by a run which saw Liverpool take 25 points from their next 15 matches. 'We shot up to second place, and Roger Hunt was in top form ... he scored 31 League goals that season'. Liverpool clinched the title by hammering Arsenal at Anfield ... and then it was on into Europe.

That was an arena in which I always felt Bill Shankly was mistrustful of the opposition. I once sat behind Bill on the team coach, going to the game during the evening rush hour. We were behind what used to be called the Iron Curtain – it was either Budapest or Bucharest – and Liverpool were about to engage the enemy in another European confrontation. We got stuck in a traffic jam because of a car that was parked just ahead. I could see Bill's neck becoming ever more red – then, suddenly, he leaped up from his seat, stalked down the aisle and ordered the interpreter to 'get that bluidy car moved!' It may have been pre-match nerves getting to Bill, it may have been fear of arriving at the ground late ... whatever, he wanted action; immediate action.

When a couple of police motor-cyclists turned up, I feared the worst – would we all be arrested? Would Bill be able to contain himself? – The young interpreter managed to explain to the police what the problem was, and suddenly there were people manhandling the car on to the footpath so that the way would be cleared for us. Bill Shankly returned to his seat, satisfied, and we reached the ground in good time.

On another occasion, when we were waiting at the airport in an East European country for the flight back to Liverpool, we were delayed for a considerable time because an incoming flight was deemed to be more important – it contained Russian military top brass on their way to Nasser's funeral, we were told, and as we stood to one side, these bemedalled visitors – including one woman – marched across the red carpet which had been rolled out for them in the transit lounge. While we were all kept waiting, Bill Shankly was making it clear, to anyone who cared to listen, just what he thought of this 'After-you' kind of treatment we were getting, and once again I began to worry and wonder if we would all be locked up, because you never felt certain about your freedom in a country behind the Curtain. Indeed, on one occasion while Bob Paisley was managing Liverpool, I travelled with the team to Poland for the match against Slask Wroclaw, and there were a couple of experiences which made you feel ready to board the plane for home at the earliest possible moment. The match was been played in the afternoon, and it was a bitterly cold day, with the temperature well below zero. Two coaches were scheduled to take the Liverpool party to the ground; one carried the team and backroom men, the other the Press and club directors.

From the moment of our arrival at Poznan airport we had the services of an interpreter – a man dressed in drab khaki whom I figured was probably from the Polish Army – and he accompianied the coach in which we were about to travel to the ground. He did a head count, and discovered that the captain of the aircraft, which was on charter to Liverpool Football Club, was missing. The rest of the crew were with us, and the first officer explained to the interpreter that the captain was still in bed, resting, and that he intended to make his own way to the airport so that he would be ready and waiting when the rest of us turned up that evening.

Immediately, the interpreter told the first officer that the captain must be summoned, and that he must travel with us to the game. 'We shall find him a bed at the ground' was the gist of his message, as he sent the first officer on his way to awaken the captain. Shortly afterwards, the two pilots emerged from the hotel and climbed aboard; we were then allowed to proceed to the football ground. I never did discover if a bed was made available for the captain, but I had an alarming experience of my own once the match had ended – as it happened, with a Liverpool victory.

We had all been warned that because of the weather, Poznan airport would be closing down at seven o'clock that evening, and so we must take care not to be late – anyone who missed the coach for the airport after the match would have to fend for himself. Needless to say, there were no late arrivals … each of us made certain that he was ready to board the coach in good time. And so we set off for the airport, with the driver racing along roads which were packed with ice and snow. It was a bit of a hair-raising ride, but we made it safely, and then we had to queue to go through the security check. As it turned out, I was the last in line. When I reached the desk, the woman behind it – she hadn't a smile for the cat – took my passport from me … and promptly, without saying one word, she disappeared. I felt a little bit alarmed as I saw the tail-end of the Liverpool party vanishing from my view, as well. Foremost in my mind was the warning: 'If you're late, you'll be left behind!' I was relieved when, a few minutes later, the woman official returned and handed my passport to me – still without a word or smile.

I was no 100-yard sprint expert, nor was I a four-minute miler … but my feet scarcely touched the ground as I raced off to catch up with the Liverpool party, and I was extremely thankful when I did rejoin my colleagues and the rest of my fellow-travellers. Hardly had I reached my seat, or so it seemed, before we were taking off; up, up and away into the wild blue yonder … and I was very grateful for the drink I was soon knocking back. It didn't bear thinking about as to what might have happened, had I been the unfortunate one to be left behind. That season turned out to be a good one for Bob Paisley and Liverpool, because they claimed the League Championship and UEFA Cup.

Bill Shankly's managerial career at Anfield ended when, for the second time, he presented the club with the F.A. Cup. He had delivered it the first time in 1965, to carve out a niche in club history, and he had delivered the League title after promotion, the UEFA Cup for the first time, and the championship trophy to go with it. In the spring of 1974 I was at Wembley to see Liverpool defeat Newcastle United, and so Shankly rounded off his career with his second F.A. Cup triumph … but as we all celebrated success at the banquet that evening, we didn't know this was Bill's swan-song in management.

When the news did break, there was a Press conference at which Shanks sat alongside chairman John Smith, who told the assembled media: 'Mr. Shankly had intimated that he wishes to retire from football'. Immediately after the shock news had been absorbed, of course, the guessing game began … who could possibly follow this man who had achieved so much success for the club? – I suspect that at that moment in time, there would not be a lot of people who would have been prepared to put money on Bob Paisley – and, if they had, they would most surely not have been prepared to bet that he would become the

Parting Gift … Bob Paisley and Chairman John Smith hold aloft the F.A. Cup, which Liverpool won for the second time, in 1974. It was Bill Shankly's parting gift to the club, as he announced his decision to retire.

most successful manager in the history of British football. Most people considered it to be virtually an impossible task for anyone who was asked to follow the previous act. Shankly and Liverpool were synonymous with each other; they went together like fish and chips, bacon and eggs, salt and pepper. They were – or, at least they had been – indistinguishable from each other. They were one and the same; you couldn't separate them. But Bill Shankly had decided that so far as he was concerned, the game was up. And Liverpool had to get on with it, without him.

Bob Paisley, being Bob Paisley, didn't give up without a fight – as he told me, he spent three weeks talking to Shanks, in an effort to persuade him to reconsider. 'I did everything I could when I talked to Bill, but it was no use', Bob said. 'He'd made up his mind to go, and that was the end of it'. And so the die was cast. But if Paisley couldn't manage to persuade Bill Shankly to change his mind, the canny Geordie himself had to be talked into stepping into Bill's shoes. And even then, when he had finally allowed himself to be talked into the job, as he told Emlyn Hughes: 'I'm here on sufferance … I don't suppose I'll be here very long'. Paisley's reign was to last from 1974 to 1983, and during those golden years he not only celebrated the 40th anniversary of his arrival at Liverpool with a championship success … he graduated with more honours than even his illustrious predecessor had done – which was saying something.

I was at the Manager-of-the-Year luncheon in London on the day that, like Shankly himself had once been, Paisley was installed as the top team boss. It was the supreme personal accolade, of course, although – as ever – Bob was not inclined to go overboard or even say a lot. But Shanks had something to say, and he said it in typical Shankly style. When he got to his feet to address his audience, we all paid attention, and his words were worth listening to. I remember his parting shot. It went like this: 'I suppose (referring to his successor's achievements, which by then included the European Cup) that you're thinking I'm feeling a wee bit jealous'. There was a pause; then Bill hammered it home as he concluded: 'By Christ, ye're bluidy right!' The words were robbed of any malice, because Bill was smiling (if somewhat wryly) as he spoke. I'll round off this chapter by quoting someone else – William Shakespeare, the Bard of Avon. He it was who wrote: 'Some are born great; some achieve greatness; and some have greatness thrust upon them'. In Bob Paisley's case, so far as those last two sentiments are concerned, I reckon it was a little bit of both.

Wall of Fame ... Bill Shankly and Bob Paisley, two of the greatest managers British football has ever seen, are pictured side by side in a place of honour at Anfield.

Memories are made of this … a reunion between Bob Paisley and his old team-mates, Billy Liddell and Phil Taylor.

CHAPTER 4

Press-ganged!

IT WAS Bill Shankly who signed Emlyn Hughes from Blackpool for around £65,000, and Em went on to captain both Liverpool and England. His career at Anfield spanned not only 13 seasons, but the managerial careers of Shankly and Bob Paisley. His extrovert, ebullient style of play earned him the title of Crazy Horse, as the Kop took him to their hearts, and he totalled more than 650 appearances for the Anfield club after his arrival in March, 1967. Shankly acclaimed him as a future captain of England, and Emlyn obliged, as he made 62 international appearances. He it was who skippered Liverpool to their first European Cup success, in 1977, by which time Bob Paisley was the manager.

According to Hughes, Paisley's great strength was in spotting weaknesses in the ranks of the opposition. 'His tactics weren't idiotic … he didn't talk rubbish', said Emlyn. A verdict echoed by Paisley's first signing, Phil Neal, who told me that both Bob and his successor, Joe Fagan, talked common sense. More of Neal later. The way in which Bob Paisley came to tackle such a mountainous task as that of following Bill Shankly is an interesting story in itself, because not only was he a reluctant hero … he almost had to be press-ganged into taking the hot seat. As Liverpool's chief executive, Peter Robinson, was to admit, the news of Shankly's decision to quit came 'as a bombshell … we were faced with the problem of what we were going to do about it'. Having finally and reluctantly accepted that they could not sway Shankly, Liverpool turned to his right-hand man. 'He said he preferred to stay where he was', said Robinson. 'Eventually, we ganged up on him'.

Liverpool's chief executive revealed that 'we talked to Joe Fagan and Tom Saunders … it was a group effort that got Bob to take the job. That's it in a nutshell – he was press-ganged. And he was still very reluctant'. But although Bob regarded himself as 'the buffer' until someone else with greater qualifications came along, he found himself in the position of having fame virtually thrust upon him. And almost immediately it became apparent that there was likely to be a problem, because Bob didn't really seem to be at ease when it came to handling the media. As racing trainer Frankie Carr had once said, when it came to handling footballers, Bob Paisley's way fascinated him; but when it came to dealing with the media, that was something else.

When Bob and I discussed his early days in the job, he looked thoughtful as he told me: 'In my first season, I tried to please everyone … then I realised that it just couldn't be done'. And right at the start, when I compiled his first programme notes, he told me: 'I know that I can never have the same rapport with the fans that Bill had. I just hope that I can let the team do the talking for me'. The Geordie with the image of woolly cardigan, cloth cap and carpet slippers was now well and truly in the firing line – but as time went by, everyone could see just how well his team did the talking for him.

The first programme notes of the season contained – naturally – a fulsome tribute from chairman John Smith to Bill Shankly. Smith declared that 'continuity and stability must be the theme', and he asked: 'Why change something that has been tried and proved, over the years?' He gave this answer, too: 'We believe we have made the right decision' … but, of course, that remained to be seen. The chairman pointed out that Paisley 'has been popular with the players … he has also commanded their respect. We see no reason why Liverpool should not go from strength to strength'. And to give Bob a boost, I featured him in another page of the programme in a piece headlined 'Yesterday's Heroes'. Bob had indicated that he was willing to serve the club 'in any capacity' – and he meant it; yet, once having taken up the gauntlet, he declared that 'the prospect doesn't daunt me'. And in his first programme notes, he referred to the close relationship he had had with Bill Shankly over a period of 15 years and said: 'There was real truth in his claim that in all that time, we never had a cross word'.

The objective was always the same – 'to do our best for Liverpool'. And that remained the objective as Bob Paisley took over at the top, with Joe Fagan, Ronnie Moran and Roy Evans all moving up a rung, as well. Bob looked back on that day when he had been persuaded by former chairman T.V. Williams to join the backroom staff … 'at 14, I'd had a year on the surface at a colliery at Hetton-le-Hole, my birthplace, then served my time as a bricklayer … and I'd probably have gone back to laying bricks'. Liverpool's new manager promised only one thing – renewed effort to achieve success. He had played his first League game for the club in August, 1946, when he lined up at left-half for the match against Chelsea, and figured in a team which came out on top … the result was 7-4. In September, 1974, mere weeks after taking charge of the side, he was seeing his men doing the talking for him as they met Stromsgodset in a European Cup-winners Cup-tie and emerge the victors by eleven goals to nil. By the end of his first season, Paisley was finding out what it took to be a successful team boss…

That record victory over Stromsgodset was a mere memory, because Liverpool had then been knocked out by the Hungarian side, Ferencvaros, in the second round (it was 1-1 at Anfield, 0-0 in the away leg, so the Hungarians went through with their away goal counting double). They had also lost at home to

Under new management … and Bob Paisley, having succeeded Bill Shankly, brings Roy Evans into his backroom team, along with Ronnie Moran (left) and Joe Fagan (right).

Middlesbrough in the League Cup, and to Ipswich at Portman Road in the F.A. Cup – each of those defeats had come in the fourth round – while in the League, Liverpool had to concede best to Derby County, who claimed the championship to leave the Anfield Reds as runners-up. It wasn't all doom and gloom, by a long way; but, as Bob admitted to me, he recognised that there were expectations of greater things next time out. So, in his final programme notes for the season, he was thanking the supporters for their loyalty (the average gate for League matches had been close on 46,000) and telling the fans: 'We shall be back – and doing our best to win something'. Few people then could have imagined the triumphs to come, as Bob Paisley steered his team to the pinnacle, both at home and abroad. Indeed, only one year later Liverpool were winding up their campaign by doing a notable double – after a very real scare.

During that first season, however, Bob had to learn how to handle the media and, as chief executive Peter Robinson was to say, in those early days that was just about the greatest problem Bob had to solve. 'Suddenly, he was in the forefront'. One of Liverpool's former players – Brian Hall, a man who had graduated with a B.Sc. degree – said that Paisley 'was not the most articulate of men … and his predecessor had been incredibly articulate. Bob said he would let his players do the talking for him'. One of those players certainly did him proud, because Phil Neal – his first signing – went on to prove that he could be classed as a recruit who gave Liverpool service equal to that which they received from the likes of Kenny Dalglish and Kevin Keegan. And Neal, like Emlyn Hughes (though he had been signed by Shankly) cost no more than £65,000 when he arrived from Northampton Town in November, 1974. He was to become a key player throughout a dozen seasons and, indeed, when Joe Fagan (Paisley's successor), decided to bow out, Neal's name was given firm consideration for the job. Peter Robinson admitted this later, after the vote had gone to Dalglish.

Bob's relationship with the media came into sharp focus, for me, when Liverpool had to play Everton at Goodison Park in mid-November, 1974. At the time, Liverpool were going through a sticky patch – they had lost, 3-1, against Arsenal in the League at Anfield, and they had been knocked out of the League Cup on home ground by Middlesbrough. These two reverses had followed Liverpool's exit from the European Cup-winners Cup at the hands of Ferencvaros and a 1-0 defeat in the League by Ipswich Town at Portman Road. November had indeed been a bleak month for Liverpool … and for Paisley. On the Saturday morning of the match at Goodison Park, Phil Neal was scheduled to play for the reserves; but instead, he found himself being told to take his boots to Goodison, and it was there that he made his debut. Liverpool emerged from that crucial game with a scoreless draw, and while they followed with three more draws in succession, at least they had started to get the show back on the road.

Not surprisingly (because the media is always on the look-out for a sensation), Liverpool's results up to that match against Everton had generated plenty of comment, and at that stage of the season, with Paisley no more than a few months into the job, Bob didn't need to be told that there was speculation about his chances of hanging on to it.

Liverpool were not noted as a club which hired and fired managers in quick succession, but they had become accustomed to seeing trophies on the Anfield sideboard, and the expectations remained high. If it wasn't crisis time for Paisley, it was becoming uncomfortably warm … at least, in the opinion of the media. And it showed, in the barbed comments some of them were making as we waited for Bob to appear, after that scoreless result at Goodison Park. He was a long time in coming, but eventually he did arrive, and his first words were to the effect that he hadn't deliberately kept his listeners waiting, and now that he was here, he was ready to answer their questions. When I reminded Bob of this occasion, some years later, and suggested that he knew the vultures had been hovering, he just smiled – but he didn't dispute what I had said. He was nobody's fool, even if people had that avuncular image of him.

Among Liverpool's results in the League that season was a 4-1 defeat by Newcastle United at St. James's Park – and that, coming as it did immediately after a 5-2 hammering of Ipswich Town at Anfield, displeased Bob Paisley. When Newcastle tried their luck at Anfield the following month, Liverpool were most certainly up for it – they inflicted a 4-0 defeat upon the Magpies, and so honour was satisfied. By the end of the season, after having stormed ahead during the early part of the campaign, Liverpool saw Derby County pip them for the League title by a two-point margin. By then, Bob Paisley had learned a great deal about the art of management, and about himself. He once summed up what winning was all about: 'When you have the advantage, that's the time to cash in. You must try to put the pressure on when you have the advantage, and not just bask in the glory of getting there'. Paisley again: 'We are often reputed to be machines, but we're realistic – if you go 3-1 up, you should try that bit harder to make sure of it. If you relax, and it gets to 3-2, you can be struggling'. And, at a time when (as usual) Liverpool were leading the field, his demand was straight to the point: 'I want more effort!' There were very few occasions when Paisley's players failed to deliver that effort and commitment … and, indeed, there were times when the team Paisley had fashioned played a brand of football which was more fluent than in Bill Shankly's day.

Shankly's teams never knew when they were beaten, and they worked hard for 90 minutes. Steve Heighway – like Brian Hall, a university graduate – once told me what, perhaps, was the scret of Liverpool's success. It was contained in a sentence of half a dozen words … 'Pass to the nearest red shirt'. In other words, don't try to complicate things – keep it simple. How often have we heard and read of people saying that, when you get down to it, football in essence really is a simple game? – Yet how often do people try and complicate things… However, even when Liverpool were still passing to the nearest red shirt during Paisley's time as a manager, there were occasions when you sensed that he had added something to their play. There was a style, a fluency that demanded admiration.

Naturally, during the reigns of both Shankly and Paisley (not to mention the eras of Fagan, Dalglish and Souness!), there were matches which lingered in the memory, and one of the games which Bob Paisley savoured to the full was a 7-0 demolition job which Liverpool did on Tottenham Hotspur. That game was played at Anfield in the first week of September, 1978, when Spurs arrived fresh from the Second Division and boasting two costly imports from Argentina – Osvaldo Ardiles and Ricardo Villa. It took no more that eight minutes for Liverpool to embark upon their scoring spree, as Kenny Dalglish struck the first goal past the unfortunate Barry Daines. Twenty minutes, and Dalglish had claimed another goal; then a cross from Terry McDermott found Ray Kennedy, and he made the scoreline 3-0. Steve Perryman headed a fierce drive from Kennedy off the line, Daines made superb saves to deny Jimmy Case and Alan Kennedy, but with the second half only three minutes old, David Johnson scored from 15 yards. It was Johnson again, for goal No. 5, after a delightful move featuring Dalglish and Ray Kennedy, and when Heighway was downed in the penalty area, Neal made no mistake from the spot. The goal which crowned the afternoon both for Liverpool and for Bob Paisley came just inside the final quarter of an hour, as Liverpool swept the ball forward in breathtaking style …

Johnson, Heighway and Ray Kennedy were the men involved, and McDermott's far-post header despatched the ball past Daines. Bob Paisley termed that goal 'one of the best in the history of the club', and he reckoned Liverpool's display was so classy that it almost defied description.

If Phil Neal had been Paisley's first recruit, Ray Kennedy had been Bill Shankly's parting gift (along with the F.A. Cup) to the club – on July 20, 1974, Kennedy had been signed from Arsenal for £180,000, and he was a player Shankly and Liverpool knew all about; because in season 1970-71, he had figured prominently in the Gunners' team which accomplished the classic double of League title and F.A. Cup … the latter at Liverpool's expense. Kennedy had been a front-line man at Highbury, but it was Bob Paisley who decided he should be switched to a left-sided, midfield role. During his eight seasons at Liverpool, Kennedy totalled almost 400 first-team appearances and rifled home more than 70 goals. He combined physical strength with a shrewd appreciation of what was required as the game progressed, and he packed a powerful shot and could win aerial duels. Capped 17 times by England, he claimed medals galore with Liverpool, and it was a tragedy when, after he had hung up his boots, this likeable man became a victim of Parkinson's Disease.

Paisley seemed to have an uncanny ability to size up the strengths and weaknesses of individual players, great ability to slot them into roles which best suited them – and the team. He might never have seemed at ease in front of the television cameras or a posse of pressmen, but nobody needed to tell him what made players tick. Ronnie Moran on Paisley: 'He knew the game inside-out, and the biggest thing for me was that he knew the players inside-out, individually. He knew the ones who were going to work hard and the ones who didn't want to work hard and who needed the most rollockings'. Moran made another point – that Paisley 'was probably 20 to 30 years ahead of his time. He must have said, 20 or 25 years ago, that in years to come players would have agents and probably carry advertising on the back of their shirts'.

Yet Liverpool's manager wasn't always right, as I discovered after one lengthy conversation with him. Our chat finally centred on two players who had graduated with university degrees and broken through to make the grade as professional footballers. Bob told me he felt that Brian Hall would go on to make more first-team appearances for Liverpool than Heighway … in fact, while Brian totalled just over 200 games and scored 21 goals, Steve clocked up more than 460 appearances and scored 76 goals.

Bob thought that Heighway's high-stepping style, as he sped down the left wing, might make him vulnerable to injury; and he also wondered if Steve, who had come into the professional game comparatively late, in his 20's, would be able to measure up to the demands when it came to competing with lads who had been with their clubs since their early teenage days. Steve himself admitted to me that when things went against him, he tended to drop his head a bit; but he battled through and lasted 11 seasons at Liverpool. Oddly enough, it was Bob's sons, Graham and Robert, who got the credit – from their Dad, at any rate – for spotting the talent of Steve Heighway. They were the ones who first made Paisley aware of the amateur footballer who was starring for Skelmersdale United, in the Cheshire League.

Bob listened to Graham and Robert, and took their advice – he went to see for himself. He returned with the verdict that 'this was the best amateur footballer I've seen'. Paisley had been an admiring onlooker as Heighway took South Liverpool apart, and when Liverpool coach Tony Waiters went to make another check, he confirmed the Paisley viewpoint. Bill Shankly went down to talk to Steve at his digs in the Midlands – he was then at Warwick University – and (after Steve had held out for a wage of £40 a week!) the deal was done and dusted. However, Bob Paisley felt that Steve 'seemed to lack belief in himself', and I recall Steve telling me he reckoned he would give professional football a year or so – then, if things hadn't gone well, he would turn his back on the game and go into teaching. However, having gained his degree as a Batchelor of Arts, he subsequently graduated as an international in professional football. And eventually, like Brian Hall, he returned to Anfield to forge a new career on the backroom side.

Like Phil Neal, Alan Hansen was a Paisley signing, and this elegant defender who had cost just £100,000 from Partick Thistle clocked up more than 450 appearances in nine seasons with Liverpool. He skippered the side, won just about all the honours, before having to hang up his boots because the toll of injuries had finally caught up with him. When I asked him if he intended to become a manager he was firm about it. 'No...' He told me he might finish up doing radio or TV work – and now, of course, he's a regular on BBC television.

'Jockey' Hansen, who captained Liverpool to a double, confirmed what others had said about Bob Paisley. 'Nothing was ever complicated. Bob would tell us to play to our strengths and exploit the opposition's weaknesses. He kept on buying the right players – for me, the biggest thing he did was when he moved Ray Kennedy from up front to the left hand side of midfield. Bob must have spotted something there, because the left side was a specialist position at Liverpool'. Hansen termed Paisley 'shy and modest ... he used to play everything down'. He also recognised that the Liverpool manager could be something of a psychologist, and a wit, on occasion. 'I was injured, and I'd been out for four or five weeks, and I was in the gym at Melwood'. Paisley walked in, and inquired how Hansen's knee was, to be told that it seemed to be going all right, except that 'it was starting to hurt me when I tried to run upstairs'. In a flash, Paisley gave his answer: 'You should have bought a bungalow, son!' Then he turned and walked away.

Like every other player at Anfield, Hansen learned a lot from Paisley. So did Phil Neal, who told me: 'When I was at Liverpool, there was total common sense about everything they did. I was never really coached, told "Do this, do that". Basically, I was asked to play to the best of my ability, and with enthusiasm. Yes, we played with passion; we wanted to win every game'. Neal also told me: 'I wouldn't say that being manager of Liverpool is necessarily the toughest or most stressful job in football – managers are all under severe pressure, and the media can make you or break you. If you manage to achieve success early on, you can carry on for a longer period of time; but all managers face the prospect of the sack, sooner or later...' Neal himself has managed Bolton Wanderers and Coventry City and, early in 1996, he was back in the game when he took charge of team affairs at Cardiff. He told me, also, that 'a lot of managers think they're strong enough to leave the worries of the job behind when they go home, but they cannot really do that'. He made another point, too. 'I don't begrudge players the money they get today, but some of them get more in a week than I got when we won the championship...' He also recalled that 'you might get the odd flash of temper from Bob or Joe (Fagan), but that was it. I remember on one occasion Joe pulled us all in and told us, "I've had a gutful of this. Come on now, pull up your socks". We went on to win the League title'.

Joe Fagan, who followed Paisley as manager, talked to me about being 'the boss' – and the pressures of the job. He admitted: 'I did have sleepless nights ... more than a few'. Joe recalled that 'things started to pile up on you; then you find it's a rather difficult job – and that's putting it mildly. How managers stick it for years, goodness only knows – I don't. I was the wrong age for being a manager (he became 'the boss' at the age of 62), but I was fresh to the job – and yes, I did want a crack at it. But the time I spent in the job was enough, at my age'. Fagan admitted: 'I did become tired'. And other people said that, as time went by, they witnessed a change in him. Joe said: 'It started to tell. There was no such thing as going to bed at night, getting your head down and sleeping through ... you went to sleep, then you awoke and began pondering upon team problems. One of the worst things was having to drop a player – I preferred to talk about leaving him out. That's something you never want to do'.

Fagan talked also about the men he followed in the hot seat. 'Bill Shankly didn't seem to show the stress he was under, but I sometimes think he put on a bit of an act when it came to telling a player he was dropped. A player used to come out of Bill's office wondering why he'd been axed when he'd just been made to feel he was the greatest player in the world! Managers do have feelings, and they don't want to drop players. But it's a job that has to be done, at times

– and that's when you don't want to get up in a morning and go into the club'.

Bob Paisley was 55 years old when he took up the challenge of following Shankly, and when I asked Bob's wife, Jessie, about the pressures of the job, she told me that her husband occasionally had sleepless nights … but that was when he was a player. As a manager, he would sometimes get what she called 'a bit ratty' and declare: 'That's it… I'm packing it in'. But the next morning he would be on his way down to Anfield, as usual. Joe Fagan told me: 'From my own experience, I would say that for Bill Shankly, Bob Paisley and Kenny Dalglish, the stress must have been great, on occasion. And that's it – full stop. You wonder how they stuck it, once you've been in the job yourself. When a manager retires, everyone wants to know why. The answer must be that he's had a fair whack at it'.

I once saw Bill Shankly looking white as a sheet and totally drained, after a dramatic European match … which Liverpool had just won. And Joe Fagan reckoned that 'success must be more stressful than failure … it's harder to live up to, once you've achieved something. With failure, yes – you get the sack; and that's stressful – but you can go home and sleep at night without thinking about this or that problem. With success, once you've done something you have to set your sights even higher, and yet the problems, of one kind or another, are still there'.

Kenny Dalglish turned his back on football – temporarily, as it turned out – after seeing his Liverpool side draw 4-4 against Everton in an F.A. Cup tie; and he left his club topping the table. Joe Fagan bowed out after having achieved an astonishing treble at the end of his first season in management, and Roy Evans was to say of him: 'I often wonder if his achievement was fully appreciated, outside Liverpool'. Evans, who finally landed the top job at Anfield, also admitted when he took the job, 'I tended to think I knew all the aspects of it … but there were far more than I thought'. And, of course, in many ways it was a totally different ball game when Bob Paisley and Joe Fagan stepped into the managerial hot seat. Nessie Shankly mused, as she expressed her belief that 'it will never be the same at Liverpool' – this was shortly after the death of Bob Paisley – while, at the same time, she added: 'But I must say that Roy is doing very well, and I'm very proud of him'. Bob Paisley would have been proud of him, too.

Presentation time, as Bob Paisley receives yet another tribute in tangible form, this time from his fellow-directors at Liverpool.

CHAPTER 5

Double Delight

YOU HAD to be there, to appreciate the drama of the occasion … the second leg of the final of the UEFA Cup, and Liverpool striving – and struggling – to win it. The match came at the end of the season 1972-73, and the emotion of the occasion was summed up by a newspaper colleague of mine as he muttered: 'If Liverpool lose this one, there's no way I'm going back on the same plane as Shanks tonight …' The first leg of that UEFA Cup final had taken place a couple of weeks earlier, at Anfield, and as Kevin Keegan scored twice and Larry Lloyd struck a third goal, it seemed to the 41,000 fans who were there that nothing could prevent their heroes from achieving the club's first triumph in Europe.

The return game against Borussia Moenchengladbach became a real cliffhanger, however; a nail-biting affair as Gunter Netzer ran the show for Borussia from midfield, and the men from Liverpool were two goals down with 45 minutes to play. It was backs to the wall with a vengeance, as Liverpool fought a tough, rearguard action. As the minutes of the second half ticked away and the tension mounted, that was when my colleague muttered those words about refusing to fly back in Bill Shankly's company, should the worst happen. Fortunately, the worst didn't happen – and Liverpool hung on to claim the trophy by virtue of a 3-2 aggregate victory. They had taken the UEFA Cup with them, and they were able to return with it as the new holders. Borussia Moenchengladbach were to figure largely again, during Bob Paisley's term as manager; and another team from the Continent caused hearts to flutter as Bob steered his team towards a double of championship and UEFA Cup. That was in his second season as 'the boss' – season 1975-76.

The campaign began inauspiciously enough, with a 2-0 defeat away against Queen's Park Rangers and a 2-2 home draw with West Ham in the League; then Tottenham Hotspur were vanquished, 3-2 at Anfield, and Leeds United fell, 3-0 away. A draw at Leicester, a home win over Sheffield United, and a 2-0 defeat at Ipswich in the League were sandwiched by a League Cup victory at York, while in the away leg of the UEFA Cup against Hibernian, Liverpool lost 1-0. There was a home win, 3-0, against Aston Villa and the Goodison derby game against Everton ended scoreless before Liverpool beat Hibs 3-1 in the Anfield return … thanks to a John Toshack hat-trick between the 20th and 65th minutes of the UEFA Cup-tie. Burnley earned a League Cup replay at Turf Moor, and applied the knock-out blow to Liverpool there, but in the UEFA Cup the Anfield Reds marched on, winning 3-1 in Spain against Real Sociedad and 6-0 in the second leg at Anfield.

In the meantime, Liverpool had beaten Wolves and Birmingham City, drawn against Coventry City away and Derby County at home, as well as scoring a 1-0 win against Middlesbrough at Ayresome Park. Manchester United went down 3-1 at Anfield, Newcastle United were beaten 2-1 at St. James's Park, then Coventry shared the points at Anfield before Liverpool went to Poland to tackle Slask Wroclaw in the third round of the UEFA Cup. It was bitterly cold, well below freezing, and the pitch was packed with ice and snow – but Liverpool had gone well prepared, with the right kind of footwear, and they were the ones who seemed to be at home on the treacherous surface. Three goals came in the second half – two of them to Liverpool – and when they got Slask Wroclaw back to Anfield, a hat-trick from Jimmy Case saw off the Polish side. However, in the League games between the two legs of the UEFA Cup, Liverpool had lost 3-1 at home to Norwich and drawn 2-2 against Arsenal at Anfield, with a scoreless draw at Burnley, for good measure. Bob Paisley used to say that of the three major European competitions, the European Cup-winners Cup was the easiest

Heading for a double ... Bob Paisley has words of wisdom for his players before they tackle Real Sociedad in Spain. That was in October, 1975 – and by the end of the season Liverpool had lifted the UEFA Cup and the League-championship trophy.

to win, while the old Fairs Cup (which became the UEFA Cup) was 'much harder than it appears … with a rapid turnover of clubs, there is always some new and unknown quantity'. There were also more matches to play – and yet Liverpool triumphed in this tournament, while missing out on the Cup-winners Cup.

During the trip to Poland, one man got a close-up view which, at one time, he could never even have dreamed about; another fan demonstrated the kind of loyalty to Liverpool which was well above and beyond the call of duty; and two of Liverpool's supporters in Poland itself – and there were many, as I discovered during the years when I edited the club's match-day programme – were rewarded for their loyalty, if only in a very small way. The Polish fans visited the team's hotel on the morning of the game, and as I watched them enter, I thought they had travelled from Merseyside. It was only when one of them spoke to me that I realised they were home-based, but they intended to cheer for Liverpool that afternoon. They had managed to get tickets for the match, but there was one little thing they would have liked … and that was some English cigarettes. When they offered me one of their own brand, how could I refuse to hand over a full packet of the brand which I smoked?

The Liverpool supporter who demonstrated his devotion to the club also turned up in time for the game – and he hadn't got a ticket. Needless to say, when we heard his story, we made certain that he was able to get to the ground and through the turnstiles there. He had indeed gone to a great deal of trouble to see his favourites in action, on that freezing-cold Wednesday afternoon. His visa had not arrived until the previous Friday, just in time for him to catch an overnight coach from Liverpool to London; and then he travelled on, by train to Harwich, by boat to the Hook of Holland, by train once more to Hanover and Berlin, where he went through what, in those days, was known as Checkpoint Charlie. Having entered East Germany, as it was then, he boarded yet another train, which took him to Kunowice and, finally, on to Wroclaw … where he arrived just a few hours before kick-off time. And that was when I heard his story.

No doubt he was overjoyed to be there and see Liverpool win, but he hadn't much time to stay around for any celebrations. Like us, he had to be on his way home – only while we flew back, he did it the hard way, once again. A taxi took him back to Kunowice for the last train of the day, which left at eight o'clock in the evening; then he retraced his journey back to Liverpool. All in all, he had spent almost a week travelling, just to see his favourite team in action for 90 minutes.

That was Liverpool's first-ever visit to Poland, and – since any trip behind the Iron Curtain meant a venture into the unknown, to some degree – the club wanted as much information as possible. More than that – while the Poles probably wouldn't understand Bob Paisley's Geordie accent, Bob himself would feel much happier if he had an interpreter to rely upon. He found one right on the club's own doorstep. What was more, the man in question, John Conrad, was a season-ticket holder … and he had been born in Poland. He volunteered for the job of interpreter, and for his pains he got a ringside view of the game – because he sat alongside Bob Paisley and Liverpool's backroom team, on the bench. His story was worth the telling, too, as I found out when I talked to John.

During the early days of the second world war, he and his family had been moved to Siberia. John was aged around 12, at the time. By 1946, however, he was finishing up in England, after some years and experiences which must have been difficult, to say the least, at times. Once in this country, he went looking for digs, and he found them in Birkenhead, just across the river from Anfield. He told me: 'When I asked my landlady, in my fractured English, where I could go to see a football match, she told me to catch the ferry boat across the River Mersey, then follow the crowd … and I finished up at Anfield. I became a Liverpool supporter that day, and remained one ever since'. And that was how John Conrad not only found himself back on native soil, but giving Liverpool and their manager the benefit of his knowledge. John Conrad, I might add, didn't do so badly, either, in his adopted country … he became a director of a company which had a chain of more than 50 fashion shops in the Merseyside area.

That match in Poland was played during the last week in November, 1975, and by the end of the year, Liverpool had strung together an impressive run of victories in the League, as they awaited their next venture in the UEFA Cup. After the 3-0 win over Slask Wroclaw at Anfield, Spurs felt the draught of a 4-0 thrashing at White Hart Lane, Queen's Park Rangers went down 2-0 at Anfield, and a 1-1 draw away against Stoke City was followed by a lone-goal victory over Manchester City at Anfield. Then Liverpool kicked off in 1976 by knocking West Ham out of the F.A. Cup with a 2-0 win at Upton Park.

There was a thrilling draw with Ipswich Town at Anfield, as the sides shared half a dozen goals, a scoreless result against Sheffield United at Bramall Lane, then Liverpool suffered the knock-out blow themselves, as they lost, 1-0, in the fourth round of the F.A. Cup against Derby County at the Baseball Ground. West Ham were made to suffer for that reverse, though, as Liverpool returned to Upton Park for the League encounter, and rattled in four goals without reply. Leeds United were beaten 2-0 at Anfield, Manchester United were held to a 0-0 draw at Old Trafford, and Newcastle United lost 2-0 when they tried their luck at Anfield. By then, it was the third week in February, and a date was looming with Dynamo Dresden in the quarter-finals of the UEFA Cup. But first, Arsenal and Derby County had to be met and mastered. However, Liverpool went down at Highbury by the only goal of the game, then they managed a 1-1 draw at the Baseball Ground.

The next item on the agenda was another trip behind the Iron Curtain – to Dresden, a city famed for its beauty before it was virtually destroyed by bombing during the second world war; and, of course, it had not been given much chance to recover during the occupation by the Russians in post-war years. Yet Liverpool were to find plenty to be pleased about from their trip to Dresden, for they prevented the East Germans from scoring, even if they didn't manage a goal themselves. However, a home reverse in the League, as Middlesbrough won 2-0 at Anfield, came as a bit of a shock, although the next match produced a 1-0 victory away, against Birmingham City. And so the stage was set for the return match against the team from East Germany, and goals from Jimmy case and Kevin Keegan saw Liverpool through, on a 2-1 aggregate. At that stage, with the UEFA Cup semi-finals coming up and the race for the League championship still to be won, Liverpool still had everything to play for – and play for it they did. Norwich City were beaten 1-0 at Carrow Road, Burnley lost 2-0 at Anfield … then Liverpool had to travel to Spain to take on Barcelona in their famous Nou Camp stadium, where 70,000 partisan fans filled the arena and prepared to roar their favourites to victory … except that, at the end of 90 minutes, it was Liverpool who had triumphed, by the only goal of the match. It was scored by John Toshack, after 13 minutes – unlucky 13, as it turned out, for Barcelona.

That result, without doubt, was a famous victory – but in the League, there was a 'toughie' straight away … the derby game against Everton; and then, before the Anfield return with Barcelona, a home match against Leicester City and a trip to Villa Park. The chase for the title was just as tantalising as the quest for the UEFA Cup. Liverpool met Everton on April 3 – F.A. Cup semi-final day – and emerged from the encounter the victors by the only goal; then they claimed a 1-0 win over Leicester, and achieved a scoreless draw against Aston Villa. So it was a case of 'Bring on Barcelona at Anfield…' And that second leg of the UEFA Cup semi-final certainly produced a few heart-stopping moments. At half-time, the game hadn't produced a goal – but after five minutes of the second half it was Phil Thompson, never noted for being a marksman, who had the Liverpool fans cheering. And though Barcelona put up a fighting display and scored a goal themselves, that precious strike from Toshack in Spain meant the difference between Liverpool marching into the final or making their exit from the European tournament.

It was the middle of April and, as usual, the fixtures were coming thick and fast, with Liverpool facing half a dozen games up to the end of the season. As for the fans, they were rolling up in their thousands … 54,632 for the derby game at Anfield; 44,250 at Villa Park; 55,104 for the second leg against Barcelona;

and 44,069 when Liverpool met Stoke City at Anfield. It was a game of eight goals – and Liverpool struck five of them. Two days later, Liverpool had to travel to Maine Road, and there – in front of more than 50,000 fans – they finally cruised through by virtue of a 3-0 victory. Three games to go, and every single one of these vital for Liverpool – on the results of those matches hung the destination of the League championship and the UEFA Cup. Liverpool's final match in the First Division was against Wolves at Molineux, and it was sandwiched between the two-legged final of the UEFA Cup. For Bob Paisley, this could be termed as a case of 'This is where I came in…' He had been an amateur who attracted the interest of Wolves, at the outset of his playing career (the Midlands club missed out when it decided he was too small), and in season 1946-47 Liverpool had pipped Wolves for the title. Now Paisley was set to return to Molineux for another title tilt – this time out as Liverpool's manager.

As the Liverpool players looked ahead, they knew, like their manager, that it would all come good – or all fall apart – in the space of 270 minutes. And when the players of FC Bruges, from Belgium, arrived at Anfield for the first leg of the UEFA Cup final, the home supporters and their team suffered two devastating blows. Liverpool would have preferred to be playing this first leg on the ground of their opponents – especially when they realised what was happening on their own midden – but the pattern of the campaign had been broken when the Reds were drawn at home first. In what seemed to be no time at all, the home fans were left speechless by the way the Bruges players not only went at the home side, but had the audacity to score two goals. Raoul Lambert and Julian Cools were the villains of the piece, and there were some glum faces around Anfield when the referee blew for half-time and Liverpool were still two goals down.

Two things turned the match in Liverpool's favour – Bob Paisley's half-time decision to change the tactics, and the team's own, gritty determination to make amends for having conceded those shock goals. It was Toshack who made way for Case as the game restarted … and it was Case who was to become one of the Liverpool heroes during a frantic second half. The crowd settled down as play began again, and for a short spell there was not much for the home supporters to cheer about. Just inside the hour, Anfield became a cauldron of sound as Kennedy struck for the home side … and one minute after the hour, the Anfield roar became a crescendo, because Case had put Liverpool level. They still had to worry about those two goals Bruges had scored; they still had to strive to get on top and score at least one more goal; and they still had to face up to 90 minutes of action in Belgium. But now, at least, Liverpool lived in hope. And only three minutes after Case had equalised, it was Keegan who strode up to take a penalty and slot the ball past the Bruges 'keeper. That was how the scoreline stayed, so Liverpool emerged, shaken but unbowed, the winners by the odd goal in five. It remained to be seen if they could survive and then conquer when they travelled to Bruges for the second leg. And the crowd of close on 50,000 which had witnessed that stirring comeback at Anfield debated this point as the fans trooped away from the stadium. Had Liverpool done enough?

Not surprisingly, along the corridors of power at Anfield that evening, the after-match inquests were being conducted, and when I talked to chairman John Smith about the drama of the match, he agreed that Liverpool had been a shade fortunate to turn things around – in fact, he breathed deeply, then told me: 'At half-time, after what had happened in the first 45 minutes, I'd happily have settled for a draw'. He wasn't the only one who felt that way – but, for the moment, Liverpool could forget all about the return game and what might (or might not) happen in Belgium. They had a date with Wolves at Molineux, and that was where their fate in the chase for the championship would be decided.

On the evening of Tuesday, May 4, the Liverpool team travelled to the Midlands for this vital match, and Molineux was packed with people and buzzing with eager anticipation, with the Liverpool contingent of supporters there in force and hoping their side would get the right result. It was a tense occasion for both teams, since Wolves were right down the First Division table – third from bottom, and scrapping for survival. At the top, it was Queen's Park Rangers, whose record after 42 games showed that they had finished with 59 points. Two dozen victories, 11 draws, seven defeats; 67 goals in their favour, with 33 against them. Liverpool, with this final, crucial match to be played, had won 22 games and drawn 14; they had scored 63 goals and conceded 30; and, of course, they trailed Rangers by a single point. In third place were Manchester United, also with one game to go – but four points adrift … so they were out of it, no matter what. Wolves? They were looking down on only two clubs; Sheffield United at the bottom, on 21 points, and Burnley, who had completed their programme, and who had totalled 28 points.

Wolves had reached the 30-point mark, and they were looking to round off their season not only with a victory, to salvage their First Division status, but also to deny Liverpool the championship. And it seemed very much as if they would manage to achieve both these objectives, too, when they forged ahead, as former Burnley player Steve Kindon struck. From then on, Molineux was certainly no place for faint-hearts!

Half-time came and went, and still Wolves held on to their slender lead; and as the minutes ticked away, it did begin to appear as if Liverpool were about to falter and fade from the championship race. The game had just gone into the last 15 minutes when, for the first time, Liverpool gave their fans a chance to raise the roof – and they did it again … and again. Three goals came in those final 14 minutes, and they were all scored by the men from Anfield. The marksmen? – Keegan, Toshack and Kennedy … a trio who emerged as the heroes of the night as Liverpool finally wrapped their hands around the championship trophy. Bob Paisley was back at Molineux, this time savouring success as a manager. And now there was just one game to go, as Liverpool sought to finish off the season with a memorable double. It was just like the climax to season 1972-73, when Bill Shankly had seen his players wind up with the title trophy and UEFA Cup. On that occasion, as Liverpool clinched the title with a 0-0 draw at Anfield, I had been in Peter Robinson's office after the match when in walked Bill. He marched straight to the phone, picked it up and dialled … then he spoke: 'We've done it, Nessie … there's nae-one can catch us now!'

Liverpool's players, managed by Bob Paisley, had done it, too, that night in May, 1976 – and now they were being challenged to emulate the feat of the side which, in 1973, had taken the UEFA Cup to Anfield, put it on the sideboard and savoured the pleasure of seeing it alongside the League-title trophy. There had been plenty of drama in that 1973 UEFA Cup final, especially in the second leg in Germany; and now Liverpool were all set to travel to Belgium and see what they could do. In 1973, Shankly's Liverpool had gone leading 3-0, and just squeezed through on a 3-2 aggregate; in 1976, Paisley's team was travelling in hope and with a 3-2 lead … slender enough, in all conscience, when you considered that there remained 90 minutes to get through, and on foreign soil. The two goals Bruges had scored at Anfield could yet turn out to be decisive, if away goals came into the final equation. And when the referee – Rudi Gloeckner, from East Germany – blew his whistle after 11 minutes to signal the award of a spot-kick to the home side, it seemed as if Liverpool's fate was about to be sealed. Up stepped Lambert, one of Bruges' marksmen in the first leg at Anfield, and he despatched the penalty kick past Ray Clemence.

Inside five minutes, however, the fans who travelled from Merseyside were making themselves heard in no uncertain fashion – because Liverpool were level, and so once more they held the lead on aggregate. They had been awarded a free-kick, and it was skipper Emlyn Hughes who moved forward to take it. He pushed the ball square for Keegan to try his luck – and the ball flashed from Keegan's boot to whizz past home 'keeper Jensen. From that moment on, Liverpool relied upon all their experience of European competition, as they blocked the way to goal. This time out, they were not pushing forward in the desperate hope of coming from behind, as had happened at Anfield; this time out, it was a case of foiling Bruges … who, with time running out, became ever more aware of the urgency of the situation. But, finally, referee Gloeckner's whistle was signalling that this was it – the game was over, and so the destination of the trophy had been decided. Liverpool had done the double; they were the champions of their own domestic competition, and they had carried off one of

Europe's most prestigious prizes, as well. After only two seasons, Bob Paisley had emerged as a manager in his own right; a manager whose deeds could be ranked alongside those of his predecessor, Bill Shankly.

From Shankly came this tribute to the players, and to his former right-hand man: 'It's a great moment, a proud moment'. And from the modest Geordie who had never really wanted to become the man in the hot seat came this typical salute to others, rather than priase for himself: 'It has been hard work; the lads have put so much effort into it … and what we've got, we've earned. Bill Shankly set such a high standard with great players, and I would like to think he tutored me, too. We have played a lot of games, but Liverpool have been geared to this sort of thing for 15 years. I have just helped things along'. Liverpool, indeed, had totalled no fewer than 59 matches that season – and this, despite having made their exit from domestic Cup competitions at (for them) a relatively early stage. As Paisley said, his team had played a lot of games, though Liverpool had been geared to this kind of challenge during the past 15 years. He was not to know, then, that in the very near future he and his players would carry off Europe's most prized trophy of all, the European Cup; nor that they would go so very close to claiming what would have been an astonishing treble.

The Pride of Anfield … and the trophies won at home and abroad say it all.

CHAPTER 6

The Road To Rome

LIVERPOOL totalled 61 matches during season 1976-77 and, along the way, they pulled in the crowds as they collected the trophies. It was, probably, the most memorable season of Bob Paisley's spell as a manager – even though the F.A. Cup eluded him. He and his team, and the fans, had to be satisfied with just a couple of baubles – the League title trophy, and the European Champions Cup. The F.A. Cup? – That went to Manchester United after a compelling duel with Liverpool at Wembley. My enduring memory of what, in effect, was a lost week-end, remains the spectacle of the manager and players as they recovered from their setback and prepared to set off for Rome. More of which later…

The season began for Liverpool with a 1-0 home win over Norwich City and a similar scoreline away against West Brom. Full points, so far – but away against Birmingham, Liverpool became unstuck, as the Blues won by the odd goal in three. At Anfield, West Brom appeared for a League Cup-tie and drew, 1-1, and they won the return by the only goal. So that was one trophy gone. But in the League, Liverpool scored three times against Coventry City at Anfield and against Derby County away, although when they met the Irish League part-timers of Crusaders in the first leg of the European Cup at Anfield, there was general disappointment that Liverpool managed no more than a couple of goals. Tottenham Hotspur were despatched, 2-0, on home ground, and after Liverpool had lost away to Newcastle, they travelled to strife-torn Belfast for the return match against Crusaders.

There was barbed-wire fencing, and security was tight, but Liverpool made light work of that European trip, as they scored a nap hand of goals without reply. Middlesbrough and Everton were scheduled to visit Anfield in the League before Liverpool had to play in Europe again, and a 0-0 draw against Boro' was followed by an encouraging, 3-1 victory over Everton to set the Reds up for a trip which was very much into the unknown … their first visit to Turkey, and an encounter with a team few people had even heard of. Trabzonspor. Bob Paisley struck a warning note about this one… 'We must be wary', he declared. And he was so right. Liverpool were on a high, because their dazzling display in the derby game had propelled them to the top of the First Division table – but they certainly didn't want to be brought down to earth by the Turks.

As it turned out, this was the longest distance Liverpool had had to travel on any of their European safaris, because Trabzonspor was not Istanbul or Ankara, but a remote township not far from the Soviet border. It meant nothing less than a round trip of 5,000 miles – and, of course, there was concern about the team's hotel, the food, the climate and any other conditions you might care to consider. Any hopes that Trabzonspor would agree to play in Istanbul or Ankara vanished with the news that they intended to play on their own pitch, and when Tom Saunders returned from a spying mission, his verdict did little to set Liverpool minds at rest. His trip took five days, and the report on accommodation was far from inviting, for starters. The only good thing was that Liverpool had learned, at first hand, what they could expect to encounter.

The Trabzonspor ground held around 13,000 fans – not that there would be many from Merseyside among them – and the pitch did have some grass on it; but it was of poor quality. As Manchester United were to discover in later years, the Turkish supporters were almost fanatical in their zeal for their team to succeed, and they were proud that they had seen their heroes take the place of top clubs as champions of Turkey. While Liverpool still knew little about the opposition, the Turks had plenty of information about the Anfield Reds, whom they had seen on television. They even had photographs of Liverpool players on sale in the local shops. And so Liverpool embarked upon their journey into the unknown.

They took with them an hotelier who would act as their adviser on the food to be eaten, and the journey began with a five-hour flight to Ankara, the capital of Turkey. After an overnight stop, the following day would bring a 500-mile slight on a smaller jet to Trabzon, with the match sandwiched in between a two-night stopover. Then, on day four, it would be back to Ankara to board their Aer Lingus flight for home. In the early afternoon of Monday, October 18, 1976, the Aer Lingus charter flight lifted off from Speke airport, and as he sat in the plane, Bob Paisley mused about the forthcoming test for his team. He had not only sent Tom Saunders into the lion's den, as it were; he had taken the chance to get some first-hand information from a man who had been coaching in Turkey – Arthur Cox, then the manager of Chesterfield – and he had gone to Malcolm Allison for advice, as well. Allison, like Cox, had experience of football in Turkey.

Paisley, could remember the day in 1968 when Manchester City had been pitched against a Turkish team – a side of so-called no-hopers by the name of Fenerbahce. Trabzonspor were regarded in a similar light – unknowns with very little chance. But Malcolm Allison, who in the 1960's had helped to steer City to glory at home and abroad, had discovered he was in error when he forecast that City would 'terrify Europe' – in the event, it was Fenerbahce who dished out the shock treatment and forced Manchester City to make an ignominious, first-round exit from the European Champions Cup. Paisley certainly didn't want his Liverpool lads to suffer a similar fate, and as he recalled the deeds of Fenerbahce, he warned: 'There are no easy games in the European Cup'.

Liverpool, with all their experience, were to discover yet again the truth of Paisley's words as they tried conclusions with Trabzonspor. As he had said, this match was going to 'test the players to the limit'; and so it proved. Liverpool, who had been met by the media, including television, on arrival in Ankara, had not exactly been granted lavish training facilities, and when they took to the skies once more, bound for Trabzon, they faced more anxious moments – not least when they realised that the airstrip upon which they were due to land was perched upon a plateau which stood above the sheer cliff face…

This was the reason the giant jet planes were unable to land at Trabzon, and there was a further shock for the travellers from Merseyside when, at the end of the runway, a brick wall came into view. But they got down safely, and once again turned their thoughts to the job in hand. The first thing they were asked was whether or not the kick-off time should be amended, because of the light. It was scheduled for three o'clock in the afternoon, but now the talk was of a 2:45 kick-off. However, when it came to the day itself, there was no change to the kick-off time, and the light didn't appear to present any problems. The Liverpool party travelled along roads in Trabzon which, to say the least, were bumpy, as well as winding, and on the way from the airport to the hotel the outlandish aspect of their trip was highlighted as they saw a sign containing an arrow. The arrow pointed down a side road, and the sign consisted of just one word: Iran.

When Liverpool did arrive at their destination, it was to discover that they had been switched from one hotel to another – and, as Tom Saunders had reported earlier, Trabzon contained only two hotels, to start with. One of these – the better one, believe it or not – did not possess a restaurant, nor did it provide facilities for meals, while the second hotel, catering for clients, was not so hot. Paisley was clearly annoyed when he realised what had happened, and he declared their accommodation to be 'a doss house'. Indeed, he added that this accommodation for Liverpool's finest was 'the worst I've known since I was in the desert', and he reflected that the Turks had been 'very naughty' to switch their guests from one hotel to the other. But, of course, there was nothing to be done about it, and the canny Geordie tried to use the situation and turn it to his team's advantage. Once upon a time Bill Shankly had told his players that they were up against the finest team in Europe – and this, after they had just beaten Anderlecht. Now Paisley told his men there was only one thing to do – go out and give the Trabzon team a good hiding. Easier said than done, though, as Liverpool were to discover. Meanwhile, their manager cooled down, while reminding his players that they would be striving to restore British pride. He also told the media that the Turks, basically, seemed to be decent enough people … it was just that everything seemed to have gone wrong since their arrival.

While Jack Ferguson, the hotelier who had travelled with the team, was occupied with keeping a constant check on the food the players were eating, the club doctor was dispensing pills and potions designed to keep them on top line and prevent them from going down with stomach bugs and the like – and Bob Paisley was keeping his fingers crossed that Ian Callaghan, one of Liverpool's most experienced European campaigners, would have recovered from an attack of fibrositis. 'Cally' was able to line up for the kick-off, though Phil Neal – another who so seldom missed a match through injury – had to drop out, which gave Tommy Smith a chance to take over at right-back.

Just before the game began, a local beauty who had won a Miss Turkey competition arrived on the pitch to provide a touch of glamour as she supposedly kicked-off, and then the battle began for real, as referee Nicolai Rainea, from Rumania, got the game under way. Trabzonspor had become the first provincial club to wrest the championship from the big-city giants in 18 years, and they showed that they intended to make the most of their moment of fame. They were fortunate, for a start, in that the tremendous amount of travelling had left some of Liverpool's players feeling a little bit limp, although by half-time neither side had managed a goal. The Turks had been restricted to a couple of moments when they spelled danger – with a header, and with a drive which went over the bar – but about 15 minutes after the restart Liverpool's luck was well and truly out as they conceded a goal. The referee ruled that Emlyn Hughes had impeded Necmi as he passed the ball back to Ray Clemence, and though Liverpool protested that they were being penalised harshly, the verdict was a spot-kick. Even then, the Turkish captain, Cemil, needed a spot of luck as he sidefooted the ball towards Liverpool's goal – instead of making contact cleanly, he seemed to miskick. As Clemence dived in one direction, the ball hit the post … bounced off it, and crossed the line on the side opposite to where the 'keeper had dived. Clemence suffered again, too, as he became the target for stones thrown from the crowd. Twice in the second half Liverpool had scoring efforts cleared off the line, but the final score remained 1-0, with Paisley declaring that the trip had been 'a disaster from start to finish'. As for the ball, he reckoned this had been 'a pig's bladder'.

So Liverpool, already leg-weary, set off for home, and they had to tackle Leeds United only 48 hours later. They emerged from this Elland Road contest with a point, won 1-0 against Leicester City at Filbert Street, and scored three goals without reply against Aston Villa at Anfield. That brought them up against Trabzonspor again, and when the match went on at Anfield the Turks had more than a few vociferous fans cheering for them. This time out, however, Liverpool were more than a match for their opponents – three goals inside a dozen minutes of the first half killed the game as a contest. Steve Heighway scored after eight minutes, David Johnson after 10, and Kevin Keegan after 19. So the 42,000 fans went home happy, and Bob Paisley could sit back and reflect that his players could now concentrate on the League for a while. The next European outing would not be until early March, when Liverpool would come up against St. Etienne – the French team known to their supporters as Les Verts ... The Greens.

Three wins and a draw followed that 3-0 victory over Trabzonspor, with Leicester City being hammered 5-1 at Anfield, Sunderland losing 1-0 at Roker Park, Arsenal dropping a home point and Bristol City going down 2-1 at Anfield. December started with a 1-0 defeat at Ipswich, then a 3-1 home win over Queen's Park Rangers was overshadowed by a 5-1 reverse at Villa Park and a 2-0 defeat at West Ham's Upton Park ground. Stoke City suffered at Anfield, though, as they went down 4-0, and in the last match of 1976, Liverpool drew at Maine Road. The first month of 1977 saw Liverpool winning their third and fourth-round games in the F.A. Cup, as Crystal Palace survived at Anfield (0-0), only to lose the replay 3-2, while Carlisle United were knocked out on the back of a 3-0 result. In between, Sunderland had been beaten, West Brom had gained a draw at Anfield, and Norwich City had won at Carrow Road. When February came round, it turned out to be a month in which Liverpool were not to suffer one defeat, although they had to settle for a scoreless draw against Manchester United at Old Trafford. But at Anfield, Birmingham City were beaten 4-1, Derby County lost 3-1 – and in the fifth round of the F.A. Cup a similar scoreline accounted for Oldham Athletic. Wembley, the League title and the European Cup were all still beckoning...

The quarter-finals of the European Cup were scheduled for March, and when the draw was made, Liverpool were paired with St. Etienne. To say the least, it was a formidable task. There was the memory of St. Etienne's appearance in the final the previous season, when they had gone down so gallantly against Bayern Munich in Glasgow. Bob Paisley himself had watched that final, and his verdict was this: 'I was impressed with the French side. Only experience beat them'. Once again, as had happened with their trips to Northern Ireland and Turkey, Liverpool were making it a 'first', with their short-distance visit to France, for such a competitive match (they had met the French club before, on a close-season tour back in 1956). If Liverpool had Keegan, St. Etienne had Dominique Rocheteau, a player who – like his Merseyside counterpart – could turn a game in a flash. The French star, aged 22, had played in the final the previous season, although he had gone on only for the last few minutes of the match – but in those few minutes he had made people remember him, because he had carved out three scoring chances which were passed up by team-mates.

Naturally, when St. Etienne returned home, it was to be given a civic reception, and more that 80,000 fans lined the Champs Elysees. Rocheteau was given a hero's welcome, and this right-winger with the flair and style of a Heighway paid his Liverpool opponent a genuine tribute, as he declared himself to have been 'very impressed with his speed and skill' – a verdict delivered after having played for France against the Republic of Ireland. Rocheteau also admired Keegan and Toshack, and when it came to Liverpool, he described them as a team which played 'as a unit', while his own style tended to be 'Latin, with more improvisation'. Rocheteau's forecast: 'If we take a one-goal lead from the first leg at home, we can win the tie'. St. Etienne had gone through both their previous rounds on the strength of single-goal victories.

Rocheteau wasn't the only star of the French side, however; they had a giant of a man in Osvaldo Piazza, and he played at the heart of the defence. One opponent had described Piazza as 'a machine … I've never played against anyone like him'. Piazza, an Argentinian international, had been nicknamed 'The Beast', and before the first leg there were plenty of quips about the outcome of a confrontation between the St. Etienne defender and John Toshack.

As it turned out, Piazza was booked in the first leg for a foul – not on Toshack, but on Ian Callaghan – so he was ruled out of the return; and Liverpool's Welsh-international striker was substituted in both legs of the tie, thanks to Achilles-tendon trouble which, as it transpired, was to keep him out of first-team action for the remainder of the campaign. Toshack, indeed, finally required an operation. As for Piazza, he had been booked when playing against CSKA Sofia in the previous round, so the yellow card he received for his foul on Callaghan meant an automatic ban. Meanwhile, as Liverpool remained on course for a unique treble, the European Cup had become all-important for St. Etienne, since they lost all chance of retaining the French championship, after a 4-0 defeat at Sochaux. By then, they languished in a mid-table position.

Even so, St. Etienne were still dangerous – perhaps doubly so, now that they were left to concentrate on Europe, and in their ranks, as well as Rocheteau and Piazza, they had Gerard Janvion, an international right-back in direct opposition to Steve Heighway; Dominique Bathenay, who wore the No. 6 jersey – and whose goal in the first leg was enough to give the French a tenuous lead – while in Jean-Michel Larque, St. Etienne had a midfield general who captained the side and was an experienced international. Their last line of defence was another international, Yvan Curkovic, with two dozen Yugoslav caps to his credit. He had come from Partizan Belgrade. St. Etienne had knocked out CSKA Sofia and PSV Eindhoven, and on home territory they believed they could account for Liverpool. One of their officials who had watched Liverpool in live action declared: 'They're good – but they're not invincible'. And they went into the first leg knowing that they had not lost on home ground for four years. They had just won away against Rennes (1-0), and they were given a further boost when, almost at the last minute, Bob Paisley had to announce that Keegan would be missing from Liverpool's line-up, because he was suffering from ligament trouble. His replacement would be Terry McDermott.

St. Etienne went at Liverpool from the start, while Liverpool played it tight, with the ball being passed back to Ray Clemence time and time again. It may not have been pretty, but it was effective, and Les Verts went in for the half-time break knowing that they now had just 45 minutes to breach the opposition's defence.

Once again, St. Etienne swept forward from the restart, and twice they got dangerously close to scoring. Finally they did manage a goal, as a cross from Rocheteau struck Clemence and rebounded out of play. When the corner kick was taken, Larque sent the ball over to the far post, where Janvion had taken up position. He struck the ball, but miskicked – yet St. Etienne's luck was in, because the ball dropped for Bathenay, who whacked it in with his left foot past the Liverpool 'keeper. By then, there was no more than 10 minutes left, and Liverpool managed to hold on without conceding what would have been a very damaging second goal. Indeed, had Heighway's luck been in they would have pulled off a draw, but his effort came back off a post.

So both sides had everything to play for, when the return game went on at Anfield, where the atmosphere on this night could truly be described as electric. I was there, so I know… If there had been tension and eager anticipation before the kick-off, the volume of sound was turned up to a crescendo mere minutes after the referee had signalled that the battle could commence – because Liverpool scored. A short corner from Heighway reached Keegan, who was waiting out on the left side of the field; and he drove an angled shot goalwards, surprising the St. Etienne 'keeper as the ball curled over him and into the net. Liverpool had their tails up, all right. But it wasn't going to be as simple as that, as Paisley's men began to realise with half-time looming and no more goals in the bag.

Five minutes after the restart, there were anxious faces all around Anfield as St. Etienne demonstrated that they could counter-attack with genuine menace. It was Bathenay who collected the ball on the half-way line, and he sped forward. He simply kept on going, then he sent a 25-yarder which dipped as it beat the Liverpool goalkeeper. Suddenly, St. Etienne were back in the driving seat; level on the night and 2-1 ahead on aggregate. Now Liverpool had to score two more goals – and they couldn't afford to lose one more. They were down to the last 30 minutes of the match and needing to throw caution to the wind, if they were to salvage success from the tie. Then Toshack made a significant contribution as he prodded a centre from Callaghan forward, and Kennedy drove a low shot past Curkovic. Just one more goal, and Liverpool could still do it. Now, however, they were down to the last 15 minutes.

Not for the first time, Paisley made an inspired substitution as he decided that Toshack had done enough, and it was time for Liverpool's Super-sub, Fairclough, to be given his head. I recall a League game at Maine Road when Fairclough was sent on to break the deadlock; he ran Manchester City dizzy, inspired Liverpool to victory as they took a giant step towards the title. On another occasion, Bob told me that at one stage he had considered trying to do a swap deal with City – his Super-sub for their England winger, Peter Barnes. Nothing ever came of that ... but at Anfield, that night against St. Etienne, Fairclough lived up to his billing. The man team-mates used to call Charlie Chaplin (he often seemed in danger of falling over as he set off on one of those gangling runs) might have been leaving it late ... there were just six minutes to go, as Kennedy drilled the ball down the left side of the field, and Fairclough latched on to it.

The St. Etienne defenders were well and truly caught out as Liverpool's lanky red-head bored his way forward in a mazy run which took him round three opponents ... then he hammered the ball low for goal, and it went past the despairing Curkovic. For the first time, Liverpool were looking like winners. It was 3-1 on the night, 3-2 on aggregate; and that was how the scoreline remained, as the referee blew his whistle for the final time. Liverpool had marched into the semi-finals of the European Cup for the second time in their history ... and now they had only to knock Middlesbrough off the Wembley trail in their next match, to reach the semi-finals of the F.A. Cup, while they were still in contention for the League championship. It all sounded tantalisingly thrilling but, of course, it would be easier said than done.

In Europe, however, they were firmly expected to dispose of their next opponents, because they were up against the relatively-unrated FC Zurich. In the F.A. Cup, Liverpool had home advantage against Middlesbrough, and they made full use of this as they saw off Boro' with a 2-0 victory. Then it was off across Stanley Park for a derby game against Everton, and a scoreless draw there was considered a satisfactory result. Leeds United lost 3-1 at Anfield, Manchester City were beaten 2-1 there, and Liverpool and Stoke City figured in a 0-0 draw at the Victoria Ground. And while all this was going on, it was also back to the European Cup – in Zurich. It turned out to be easy, as Liverpool clocked up a 3-1 success.

And, indeed, it more or less was, because Liverpool struck three more goals, this time without reply. Two from Case, one from Keegan, and that was it – they were now through to the final of the European Champions Cup for the first time in their history. More than that; they were heading for Wembley in the F.A. Cup and for the League championship, after having beaten Arsenal 2-0 at Anfield immediately prior to their demolition job there on Zurich. However, when it came to the F.A. Cup, the semi-final could not have been more difficult, because Liverpool were up against Everton, and the venue for this gripping contest was Maine Road. It turned out to be a thriller, watched by more than 52,000 people ... and to this day, Everton supporters claim that they saw their side robbed. That, however, wasn't how referee Clive Thomas saw it.

The game had already produced four goals – two to each side – when Everton drove forward, and a move involving Duncan McKenzie and Bryan Hamilton ended with the latter beating Ray Clemence. Everton fans roared their delight, Liverpool's players stood looking dejected ... until the referee ruled out the goal because of an infringement. Clive Thomas later insisted that he had been correct in his decision, yet the disappointment of the Everton players and supporters was easily understood, and – as McKenzie related to me later – when the replay was staged at Maine Road the following week, he and his team-mates were still mulling over what had happened the previous Saturday. Somehow, they couldn't summon up the kind of adrenalin required to overcome their opponents. In fact, a disputed penalty decision enabled Liverpool to get their noses in front, and from then on there was really only one team in it. Liverpool virtually cruised to a 3-0 victory, in front of another 52,000 plus crowd, and so they were in two Cup finals, with the League championship beckoning, as well. By then – it was the last week in April – Liverpool still had more than half a dozen League games to go (one of them against Manchester United, their F.A. Cup opponents at Wembley), plus a European Cup final against Borussia Moenchengladbach, the team they had beaten in the final of the UEFA Cup in 1973. The European Cup final would take place in Rome on the Wednesday evening after the F.A. Cup final. The stage was set for a dramatic climax to a season which had been full of thrills and spills.

*The man who tipped off Bob Paisley about a rookie goalkeeper called Bruce Grobbelaar
... Tom Saunders, who became an 'elder statesman' at Anfield as he followed Bob on to
the board, after having played a variety of roles for the club over many years.*

CHAPTER 7

'Inwardly, I was drunk'

LIVERPOOL had to play six games – three at home, three away – in the League, to wrap up the championship at the end of season 1976-77. Their final home game was against West Ham on Saturday, May 14, with a trip to Bristol City's Ashton Gate ground two days later. On Saturday, May 21, Liverpool would be meeting Manchester United at Wembley, then they were off to Rome to try conclusions with Borussia Moenchengladbach the following Wednesday. It was all go, and the end-of-season programme started with a home game in the League against Ipswich Town on the last day of April.

It was a game Liverpool won, though only by the odd goal in three; then they scored the only goal in the game against Manchester United at Anfield … and the title was virtually theirs. A 1-1 draw against Queen's Park Rangers left Liverpool on 55 points, with three matches left, while second-placed Manchester City had 53 points and two games to go. Ipswich were third, on 51 points, and their Anfield defeat had severely dented their title aspirations. As their manager, Bobby Robson, had told me before the match, for his team this was the crunch.

Liverpool travelled down the M6 to Coventry and came away from Highfield Road with a point, which took them to the meeting with West Ham at Anfield – and there, in front of 55,000 (with 10,000 locked out), Paisley's men collected the point which ensured that they could not be caught. There were 38,000 at the match against Bristol City – bottom of the table and doomed soon to go down – yet (surprise, surprise) Liverpool lost, by a 2-1 margin. But the result didn't matter; one trophy was in the bag, and there were two more on offer. In a 17-game run, from January 22, Liverpool had lost only twice in the League, as they powered their way not only to the championship, but to the finals of the F.A. Cup and the European Cup.

When Liverpool and Manchester United met at Wembley on Saturday, May 21, 1977, there were 100,000 peple inside the famous stadium. United were managed by the ebullient Tommy Docherty, who had seen his team suffer agonies just a year earlier, when they had been 'mugged' by Second Division Southampton, who were rated virtually no-hopers. On that occasion, a player by the name of Jim McCalliog (he also wore the colours of United during his footballing career) provided the pass which sent Bobby Stokes scampering clear of the United defence before he rounded it off by beating 'keeper Alex Stepney.

That was the only goal of the game. I also had another memory of The Doc., because during the Shankly era at Liverpool I had been at Anfield for an evening match … and there, also, was a player called Lou Macari, whom Shankly was trying to persuade to join Liverpool from Glasgow Celtic. Little Lou didn't give his answer that night – when he made his decision, he opted to join Manchester United (whose manager, Tommy Docherty, had also been a spectator at the match I attended).

When Liverpool met United at Wembley, Macari was a member of the Manchester United team, along with Stepney, the brothers Greenhoff (Jimmy and Brian), and Stuart Pearson, who had been signed from Hull City. Stepney, of course, had played for The Doc. when he managed Chelsea, and it had been a bizarre situation, with Alex having cost a then world-record fee of £50,000 … and being sold by the manager after just 112 days at Stamford Bridge. He joined Manchester United for £50,000, too, and was to claim a European Cup-winner's medal with them in 1968. By 1977, he knew all about the wheeling and dealing of his manager in the transfer market, and, in fact, there was a stage when The Doc. dropped him in favour of newcomer Paddy Roche. Roche had a nightmare spell, and Stepney – who had said he would back his own record against Docherty's judgment – regained his place. The Doc. was big enough to admit that he had made a mistake.

When it came to the 1977 final, Liverpool were doomed to disappointment and defeat, as United ran out the winners by the odd goal in three. Their goals were scored by Pearson and Jimmy Greenhoff, while Case struck back for Liverpool. It was a close-run thing right through the 90 minutes, but Liverpool just couldn't make their attacking forays pay off with another goal, and so The Doc. and his players were able to parade the F.A. Cup around Wembley, while Liverpool were left to rue the day.

Before the match, Paisley had spelled it out for his players. 'Nobody has ever approached an F.A. Cup final like we are doing … we won the championship last Saturday, yet we couldn't relax and celebrate. We knew we had to face two finals. In a way, our situation is unreal … no team in England has ever experienced anything like it before'. Paisley saw himself 'as the bus driver, trying to make sure that everyone is singing at the back'. But, as he said 'it's not easy'. And the final at Wembley amply demonstrated the point he had made. Even naming his squad was a difficult job – admittedly, it was one made somewhat easier because neither Toshack nor Phil Thompson could be considered; yet Liverpool's manager knew, from bitter personal experience, that he still had to disappoint one player, at least. In the final analysis, he named Callaghan as the substitute and the man they called Super-sub – David Fairclough – found himself on the outside looking in. Cally's experience (at 35, he was the veteran of the squad) had counted in his favour. Bob Paisley admitted: 'I feel for the one who is left out'. After all, hadn't he been the one left out when Liverpool met Arsenal in the 1950 final?

Liverpool, who had taken three League points off United that season, seemed to settle more quickly, and when Ray Kennedy powered a header goalwards, Stepney looked a beaten man; but the ball cannoned off the post and was cleared. Minutes later, the whistle blew for half-time. Five minutes after the restart, however, a goal did come … for United, as Pearson scored. Almost immediately Case rapped back with the equaliser as he drove home a fierce shot. And then the die was cast, as the balled dropped for Macari to have a go. He drilled a shot towards Clemence's goal, saw it deflected by Jimmy Greenhoff – and the F.A. Cup had been won and lost. Callaghan replaced David Johnson, as Liverpool battled for another equaliser, and with just a couple of minutes to go United hearts were in their mouths as Kennedy tried his luck. The Liverpool fans were on their feet, ready to salute a reprieve for their team … then the ball rapped the angle of post and bar, and that was that. Lou Macari, the man who had turned down Liverpool for Manchester United, had his winner's medal … but maybe, in years to come, he would have been able to look back on more medals, had he opted for Liverpool that day at Anfield. However, when I talked to Lou later, he never expressed any regrets about having made his choice.

You couldn't blame the Liverpool players and their manager for feeling choked, of course; and this was apparent as the coaches travelled from Wembley stadium to the railway station at Watford, after the match. I travelled in one of the coaches, and as we stood on the platform at Watford awaiting the train back to Liverpool, there wasn't much going on in the way of conversation. The players seemed down, and it seemed unkind even to raise your voice in more than a whisper, if you did say anything. One of the points Bob Paisley had made was that as his team went into the match that afternoon, they were bidding for a League-F.A. Cup double which had been achieved only twice before, in modern times; yet no-one seemed to consider this … the accent was all on the quest for the treble. Now it was down to Liverpool to become the first English club to carry off the European Cup in the same season that they won the League trophy.

But, of course, you could sense that after the bitter pill of defeat at Wembley, there must be a question mark about Liverpool's ability to bounce back as they headed for Rome. And that was at the back of all our minds, as the train pulled into the platform and we all went aboard. I sat in a section of the dining car which also contained many of the players, and as the waiters prepared to serve dinner the atmosphere was still somewhat funereal … as Bob Paisley had said before the final, it was all a bit unreal. Joe Fagan came walking down the aisle and, as he approached the table where Ian Callaghan was sitting, he glanced at him and just said: 'Look at Cally … the old man…' What Joe meant was that, at 35, Cally had given everything that afternoon, during his spell in the thick of the action – and we all knew that if he were chosen to play in Rome, he would still be giving everything. That was the way he was made, and Joe was expressing his admiration for Liverpool's senior player.

Ray Clemence was sitting close by, and there came a moment when he changed the atmosphere, as he picked up a bread roll and chucked it across for a team-mate to catch. 'Clem' managed a smile as he did this, and suddenly there were a few more people smiling. Meanwhile, Bob Paisley had followed Joe Fagan up the centre aisle of the carriage, clearly deep in thought; he didn't appear to be seeing anyone, as he looked straight ahead. But no matter; that light-hearted act by Ray Clemence had been enough.

You still wouldn't bet your life on it, of course, but you sensed that by the time the players lined up against Borussia Moenchengladbach they would be in determined mood, rather than apprehensive. There was still a major trophy to be put alongside the one which proclaimed Liverpool as domestic champions – the one which said they were champions of Europe … and what a night of glory it turned out to be, in Rome. On the Sunday, the players had been given a day off; on the Monday, they had trained; and on the Tuesday they were flying to Italy, with Bob Paisley able to report that 'everyone is in the right frame of mind'. The squad of 17 players included Toshack, who had missed the last two months of the season; now the question was whether or not Paisley would pitch him in, to use his aerial power as he had done in the first leg of the 1973 UEFA Cup final. For their part, Borussia had just claimed their domestic title for the third successive season.

It was estimated that more than 25,000 fans from Liverpool travelled to Rome – all roads seemed to lead to the Eternal City … starting from Wembley the previous Saturday, as I had seen myself, when Liverpool fans began their trek by car, by train and by boat. As Liverpool's squad took to the air, Paisley named his team – it would be the same side which had seen out the 90 minutes of the F.A. Cup final, plus substitutes Toshack, Fairclough, Johnson, Lindsay and McDonnell (the deputy for Clemence). But on the day of the game, Toshack broke down in training, so his place went to Alan Waddle. That setback didn't stop Paisley sounding a clarion call to his troops: 'This is the chance of a lifetime … if we don't take it, it won't be for the want of trying!'

Ian Callaghan, the 'old man' of the side, was about to play in his 83rd European match, and as he savoured the prospect he admitted: 'This is the one I've been waiting for'. He had been a winner in the League, the F.A. Cup, the UEFA Cup – but the European Cup was something special. As for Kevin Keegan, about to make this final his swan-song in a Liverpool jersey, he was living in hopes, as well. He had revealed that he wanted to move on and take up another challenge; but first he would stay and help Liverpool in their bid to lift the Champions Cup. 'I hope and pray we can do it', he declared fervently. Three years earlier, he had been a scoring hero in the F.A. Cup triumph over Newcastle United … would he round off his Liverpool career as a scoring hero again?

There was a member of Liverpool's European Cup-final side who had other, less-happy memories of that 1974 final – Terry McDermott, who along with Alan Kennedy had been in Newcastle's side. Kennedy in the future was to score the winning goal for Liverpool in another European Cup final, but right now, McDermott was the man hoping that this would be his lucky night. And while Liverpool had seen off Borussia in one final, they knew they were up against some tremendous footballing talent … Berti Vogts, for one, Rainer Bonhof for another, Uli Stielike and Jupp Heynckes, and the Danish flyer, Allan Simonsen. Bonhof was regarded by German fans as the new Franz Beckenbauer, and he almost gave Borussia the lead inside half an hour, as he bored a way through, then drove a bullet-like shot towards Liverpool's goal. Clemence looked beaten – but his luck was in, because the ball rapped against the foot of a post and, somehow, the 'keeper managed to grab it. Soon afterwards, Borussia suffered a blow when Herbert Wimmer, an international who had won close on 40 caps, was injured, and Christian Kulik was called into the action.

It was Callaghan who started the ball rolling when he dispossessed Bonhof and got Steve Heighway speeding down the right. The winger provided the dashing McDermott with a precise pass, and a right-footer from Liverpool's midfield marksman left 'keeper Wolfgang Kneib stranded. First blood to Paisley's men. Yet although Liverpool still led at half-time, it wasn't, to coin a famous phrase, 'all over'. The second half was no more than six minutes old when Borussia struck back, as Simonsen snapped up a misplaced pass, cut in from the left-hand side of the field, then unleashed a drive which Clemence could scarcely have seen. Suddenly Liverpool minds went back to the previous Saturday, and to what had happened at Wembley. This time out, it was the opposition who had equalised – now it was up to Liverpool to regain the initiative. And they did just that.

Vogts was finding that for all his renowned reputation as a man-marker, he was been driven almost to distraction by the darting Keegan, whose stamina was phenomenal. As the match wore on, indeed, those legs of Vogts were tiring, and something just had to give; but before that, there were other incidents. In one of them, Clemence was called upon to deny Stielike by making a magnificent save, as he parried a goalbound drive with his knees. Three minutes more, and Liverpool were ahead again.

Liverpool won a corner on the left side of the field, and as Heighway sent the ball across, up soared Tommy Smith to power a header past Kneib. This was indeed a moment for the Anfield Iron to savour, because after a spell when his first-team career appeared to have been put on hold, he was back and playing in his 600th game for his one and only club. He had arrived at Anfield as a 14-year-old, and he had just scored his first goal of season 1976-77. He had returned to senior action two months previously, having taken over from the injured Phil Thompson, and now he might even be a match-winner with that goal.

As it happened, it was not the end of the scoring, because once again Keegan got into the act. Earlier, he had appeared to be brought down by Vogts, but the referee ignored the shouts of Liverpool fans that this merited a penalty. Referee Robert Wurtz, from France, had simply waved play on. There was another penalty appeal, as Heighway went down under a challenge from Bonhof, and then it was the turn of Clemence to make another brave save as he came out to the edge of his penalty area and duelled with Heynckes and Simonsen, after Stielike had sent over a menacing cross. With just under 20 minutes to go, Borussia's

A permanent reminder of the 1977 European Cup-final triumph ... and it's been seen by thousands in the Liverpool Visitor Centre Museum.

efforts to raise their game were brought to an end, and this time the tired legs of Berti Vogts simply couldn't keep pace with Keegan. As the Liverpool man raced into the box, his opponent was left with little option but to bring him down – and that did finally mean a penalty. Up stepped Phil Neal, and he struck the spot-kick home. The Liverpool players danced with delight, their fans exploded with a roar, and Borussia knew that, at last, they were doomed to finish on the losing end. So it proved ... and afterwards, the Liverpool players at long, long last, were able to celebrate and let their hair down.

It was a night of rejoicing which extended until after dawn had broken, and who could deny Liverpool their moment of glory? – Yet one man remained almost aloof – or so it seemed – although after the final whistle he did embrace his players in turn. Bob Paisley declared: 'No praise can be too high for them'. It was typical of the man to give his team all the credit, as he added: 'To play like they did, after their disappointment at Wembley, speaks volumes for them'.

He made another telling point, as he said: 'It shows what great professionals they are' – and that accolade, coming from one of the game's supreme professionals, came also from the heart. Paisley, however, didn't sink in a sea of champagne – or even wallow in a bathful of the stuff ... although he could have been forgiven, had he downed a magnum or two. He reflected later: 'That had to be the best moment of my life. Inwardly, I was drunk – but I didn't take a drink for the simple reason that I just wanted to savour every moment. I didn't begrudge others their chance to celebrate, but I didn't want to feel that I'd missed one moment of it all. And what pleased me so much was the fact that our supporters, while enjoying themselves to the full, also were on their best behaviour'. There was an echo of what he had said after having steered his team to their first championship under his management... 'I'm proud to be a Liverpudlian tonight'. As for the 1977 European Cup triumph, Bob summed up: 'I wanted to have all my faculties about me; about what had been done, and about the whole day and night. It was something special'. Indeed it was.

Kenny Dalglish, who achieved so much as a player for Liverpool before eventually becoming their manager.

CHAPTER 8

Keegan and Dalglish

KEVIN KEEGAN talking … 'I've not won anything as a manager yet; but if I can win a quarter of what he won, I would consider myself very, very successful'. And from Kenny Dalglish: 'If there is someone who owes a greater debt than myself in football, I would like to meet him. The help he gave me was untold'. Two men who were referring to the fellow they had known as 'the boss' – Bob Paisley. And he was a man who had had a tremendous influence on the careers of both Keegan and Dalglish. If it was Bill Shankly who signed Keegan, it was Paisley who had the final word; and, of course, it was Paisley who decided that Dalglish was the man to follow Keegan when it came to wearing that famous No. 7 jersey at Liverpool.

John Toshack, Keegan's old sidekick at Anfield, once offered the opinion that 'I didn't think he had it in him…' and he was referring to Keegan's chances of making the grade as a manager. Keegan went on to show that, like Dalglish, he did have it in him – while Kenny, of course, had already done it twice over, as manager of Liverpool and then of Blackburn Rovers. Toshack also did say that he never had any doubts about Dalglish succeeding as a team boss. Keegan's 45th birthday celebration was marred somewhat by the news that Bob Paisley had died, and that was not surprising. After all, they had known each other from the moment Keegan had first set foot inside Anfield. It was 1971, and Keegan then – a relative unknown signed from Scunthorpe United for a mere £35,000 – was pictured kicking his heels as he sat on a dustbin. He was soon to be kicking his way to footballing fame – and doing it in the best possible way, by scoring goals, not kicking lumps out of the opposition.

By the time Paisley died, Keegan had made his mark with Newcastle the second time around, because after playing a key role in helping them gain promotion during the mid-1980's he was striving, as their manager, to land the Premiership-title trophy at St. James's Park. His verdict on Paisley: 'His record is incredible … it will never be beaten. Nobody should under-estimate how important he was to Liverpool in all capacities. Now he is dead, when people look at the things he has done, they will finally realise what a great manager he was. When Bill Shankly retired, I don't think anyone in the world wanted to take the job on. Bob didn't – he told us that on the day. But for someone who didn't want the job, he did quite well! People say you have to change, to be a manager; but he was just Bob

Paisley all the way. He had absolutely no problem getting the players to play for him and understand exactly what he wanted. He had so much humility … he leaves us with some great memories'.

Dalglish, like Bob Paisley in some respects, has often been a man difficult to understand. Whereas when Bob talked in that Geordie accent of his, you sometimes needed to translate what he really meant, in Dalglish's case, that Glaswegian accent took some comprehending, now and then. Kenny himself admitted: 'I just wish I had a better command of the English language to express exactly what I feel for the man. He was the greatest of them all. He was always very modest, but one thing is for sure – underneath, he was very intelligent, and had a great knowledge of football. He could tell if someone was injured just by seeing them walk across the room. Inside, he was also very proud of his team's achievements'. Bob Paisley himself confirmed his deep knowledge of players when he told me that he could spot what kind of an injury it was, virtually the moment one of his men went down. It wasn't said in a boastful way, either – just typical, matter-of-fact Paisley style. Bob also told me: 'When Tommy Smith went down, then you knew he was hurt'. They didn't call Smithy the Anfield Iron for nothing.

The signing of Kevin Keegan came about because, first of all, Andy Beattie kept on plugging him to Bill Shankly. Keegan was playing for Scunthorpe, down the divisions, and finally Shankly told Bob Paisley: 'Go and take a look at him'. One evening Paisley and Joe Fagan travelled across country to do just that; and what they saw soon convinced them. It took all of 20 minutes for that to happen, as the youngster skippered Scunthorpe that night.

The next morning, when Shankly asked for the verdict, Paisley said simply: 'Take him'. At that time, the thinking was that Liverpool could be signing a player to replace Ian Callaghan, whose career looked to be in decline, because he was having a hard time after a cartilage operation. Remarkably, Callaghan regained both fitness and form, and lasted six more years, while Keegan emerged as another key player in Liverpool's assault on honours both at home and abroad. At the start of the following season Keegan was pitched into first-team action as a front-line man, with Callaghan switched to the centre of midfield and, as Paisley told me: 'Both moves clicked'. Keegan had exceptional stamina, and he seemed to cover every blade of grass on the park. Steve Heighway told me: 'I don't know how Kev does it… I couldn't; or if I tried, I'd be shattered'. Keegan could go straight from a training session over to Doncaster, his home town, or to some function or other, and seemingly be as fresh as a daisy when the match came round on a Saturday. Then, for 90 minutes, he would give opposing defences a chasing.

Bob Paisley told me how, at Scunthorpe, Keegan had played on the right side of midfield – a role he didn't really enjoy – but as he and Joe Fagan watched him, they sensed that he veeered towards the left as a natural thing; and, of course, in any team left-sided players are always welcome. According to Paisley, Keegan was 'the major partner' in the double act he enjoyed with Toshack, and Kevin's pace enabled him to make up ground and be there to make the most of the service from 'Tosh', and from Steve Heighway. Toshack always threated in aerial duels, and yet Keegan himself could rise to the occasion, when necessary. Paisley rated Keegan's display in the 1977 final of the European Cup his finest ever in a Liverpool jersey, and his admiration was increased by the fact that the player refused to be intimidated. Bob explained: 'There were times when Kevin reached flashpoint, after taking a lot of stick, and then he would boil over. But in the 1977 final he kept his head and, on the night, he took Berti Vogts out of the game'. There was one notable incident, during a Charity Shield match at Wembley between Liverpool and Leeds United, when Keegan and Billy Bremner tangled and both men were given marching orders. But in Rome, Keegan never came close to reaching boiling point. However, as Bob Paisley well knew, with every minute that ticked away, it was getting closer and closer to the parting of the ways.

Kevin had made it known that he wanted to take up the challenge of proving he could succeed not just in the First Division, but in the European arena, and the European Cup final was to be his farewell appearance. Paisley told me, when we discussed the problem of replacing this human dynamo of a player: 'It was obviously going to take someone special to do that – but when someone says he wants to move on, as Kevin did, there doesn't seem much point in trying to hold on to the player, if he's going to be unhappy. The best thing to do is thank him for what he's done, and let him go, with your best wishes for his future'. And that, in a nutshell, was what Liverpool and their manager did … although, at first, it seemed as if Keegan's destination would not be SV Hamburg, but Real Madrid. Because Real's general manager arrived to meet officials of Liverpool in London and talk about a deal. However, when everything had been done and dusted, it was Real who missed out and SV Hamburg who obtained his signature – though, even then, life was not to go along smoothly during the early part of his career in Germany.

Eventually, however, Keegan was to be named as European Footballer of the Year not once, but twice; and even then he was to know the feeling of deflation as he returned to Anfield with SV Hamburg and finished upon the wrong end of a 6-0 scoreline. That was in December, 1977, when Terry McDermott was a hat-trick marksman as Liverpool ran riot in the return match of the European Super-Cup. Ironically, at a later stage, both Keegan and McDermott returned to Anfield as team-mates, this time with Newcastle United – and Liverpool stuck four goals past Newcastle, in an FA Cup-tie. Today, of course, Keegan and McDermott are together again, as manager and assistant at St. James's Park.

Bob Paisley didn't believe that Kevin Keegan became a better player by going abroad. What he did feel was that Keegan lost none of his ability, but gained in a fitness sense from having to play fewer matches than had been the case while he was starring for Liverpool. This meant that he wasn't coming under the same kind of physical pressure – a point which has been made about other players who have tried their luck abroad.

No doubt about one thing: the departure of Keegan put the onus on Paisley to come up with someone special as his replacement – although Kenny Dalglish did once tell me that he had never regarded himself as being just that. And it wasn't said in any boastful sense. Like Keegan, Dalglish was always his own man … and when Paisley had made up his mind that Dalglish was the man for him, all he had to do was persuade Glasgow Celtic to part with him. In the event, Dalglish tipped the scales by making it clear to the Scottish club that, like Keegan, he sought a new challenge; and once Celtic manager Jock Stein realised the futility of trying to keep him, the die was cast. Liverpool had collected a cool half-million pounds for Keegan … Celtic knew this, and they wouldn't settle for less than £440,000.

So what made Bob Paisley go for the Scot? – He told me: 'I'd seen Kenny playing for Scotland, watched him on television – and the more I saw of him, the more I became convinced that here was what I called a Liverpool-type player. It was his attitude to the game. He wasn't flashy; he did the simple things, and he was consistent, too. He was rarely out through injury, either. His timing was immaculate … and his head ruled his feet. When it came to finishing off a move, he was almost clinical'. Paisley recalled two matches against Ipswich Town. In the first one, Dalglish sped into the penalty area, looked up and took in the fact that Ipswich 'keeper Paul Cooper was coming from his line. That was the moment when Dalglish demonstrated how clinical he could be, with his finishing, as he calmly chipped the ball over Cooper's head and into the net. On the second occasion, almost one year later, it was Liverpool and Ipswich again; and a similar situation cropped up. This time Cooper must have remembered how he had been caught out before … he didn't come off his line to risk being chipped – but Dalglish summed up the situation, too. He simply drove in an early shot with his left foot, and the ball whizzed past Cooper.

Those were not the only times when Dalglish showed his coolness in front of goal – or even when he wasn't in direct line for a shot. He was to do a similar kind of thing in the 1978 European Cup final against FC Bruges at Wembley, when he collected a pass from Graeme Souness out on the right; then he looked goalwards and, as the Bruges 'keeper advanced, Liverpool's Scottish striker lofted the ball over him. That goal kept the European Cup at Anfield.

Kevin Keegan himself reckoned that Dalglish had been 'the best Scottish player for the last four years ... he's such a good player, he would fit in anywhere'. That was a verdict once echoed by Jock Stein. Keegan said he and Dalglish were 'completely different, with different qualities', and that was true enough, to a degree. Keegan was the darting, bustling type of player who could be like quicksilver, at times; Dalglish was the more studious footballer, not exactly a Powderhall sprinter, yet a player whose positional sense enabled him to be there when it mattered. Keegan summed up: 'What we have in common is a desire to see the ball in the back of the net, whether we put it there or help one of our team-mates to do the job'. And he was certainly right about that – both men were team players; both men were also swift to size up – and to seize – a scoring opportunity. In 321 appearances for Liverpool, Keegan totalled a century of goals; as for Dalglish, he eclipsed that tally, both in appearances and goals scored.

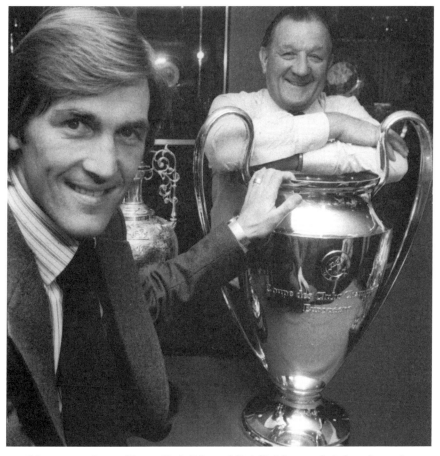

It's ours again ... Kenny Dalglish and Bob Paisley get their hands on the European Cup, after the 1978 triumph against FC Bruges at Wembley.

By season 1985-86, when he was about to hang up those shooting boots of his, Dalglish had struck 160 goals in 470 games for Liverpool – and, overall, became a 300-goal marksman during his career.

Keegan rated Dalglish as being similar to himself, in that he was 'fortunate to be a key player in a tremendous team. Each of us happens to occupy a vital position where our strengths could be seen to play a part in the success of the team. Each of us takes more than his share of responsibility, because of the position in which we play. I need not to be restricted, and I respond by doing my utmost. I think Kenny is exactly the same. He is the complete team player'. And when I discussed this point with Dalglish, he told me he didn't see himself just as a scorer of goals ... he saw himself as a team player. Keegan made the point, too, that neither he nor Dalglish missed many games because of injury – 'yet that's not because we've been afraid to go in where it hurts'.

If Kevin Keegan was able to call that 1977 European Cup final in Rome 'a fairy-tale ending to what had been a fairy-tale career with Liverpool', Kenny Dalglish was also able to look back upon his career at Anfield with satisfaction, not least because he followed up success as a player by achieving so much as a manager. When Keegan talks about 'going in where it hurts', I have a memory of Dalglish walking from the pitch with one hand clasped to his cheek – the cheekbone had been fractured in an accidental collision with Kevin Moran, who at that time played at centre-half for Manchester United. Dalglish was out for several weeks, and a surgeon to whom I talked about the injury told me: 'It can be relatively simple to get the cheekbone right – but there might be a psychological reaction once the player comes back and has to go up to head the ball. At the back of his mind there might be the fear of getting another injury like that'. Dalglish did come back, to demonstrate that he was not going to chicken out of challenges, and to show that he could carry on making and scoring goals.

Emlyn Hughes said he believed that Dalglish was one of only two players (Trevor Francis was the other) who could have replaced Keegan at Liverpool. 'Kenny seems to "get lost" – you think you've held on to him, and the next minute he's free and sticking the ball into the net. He can lose markers very easily'. Hughes said that for Paisley to land Dalglish, when he had just lost one of the game's finest players, 'was a master-stroke ... no-one thought we could replace Kevin Keegan, but if anything, Kenny was a better club player than Kevin'. Yet Dalglish did say to me: 'I'm not trying to take over from Kevin – I'll just try to be my own man'. The size of the fee didn't worry him – 'I don't have to carry a price tag on my back ... just play to the best of my ability'. And that ability was considerable because, as Bob Paisley said: 'By signing him, we've got one of the best players – if not the best player – in Britain. He has so much ability, and he can play in any position, as all good players can'.

According to someone who had come up against Dalglish at the highest level – England and Liverpool goalkeeper Ray Clemence, who during his own career clocked up 1,000 appearances since he started out with Scunthorpe and ended up with Tottenham Hotspur – Dalglish always impressed with his work-rate, while his strongest asset was that 'he can go late from midfield and finish up with a tremendously accurate shot – something a lot of forwards don't do. When Kenny gets into a scoring position, almost always he forces the 'keeper to make a save'. Dalglish, who was 'a bit nervous, but not overawed' when he kicked off with Liverpool, declared that 'the main thing that gives you confidence is if the manager keeps picking you, week after week'. There was no danger that Bob Paisley would fail to keep on doing that.

Dalglish soon discovered what, for him, was Liverpool's strong point. 'I've found that at Anfield it's a case of taking each game as it comes, and everyone plays for each other. So that makes Liverpool a difficult side to beat, and that's the team's biggest strength'. And as he looked forward to playing in the final of the European Cup, at the end of his first season with the club, he wasn't talking about his prospects of being the match-winner (which he was, as it turned out), but saying rather that if he did round off the season by claiming a winner's medal 'it will have been the team effort that made it possible'. Bob Paisley was always reluctant to make comparisons between Kevin Keegan and Kenny Dalglish, though he did tell me: 'If Kevin had greater speed and physical strength, Kenny has the speed of thought which gives him the ability to read every situation. The goal he scored at West Brom in season 1978-79 was a case in point'. Paisley reckoned that no other player would have realised there was even a half-chance of sticking the ball in the net, because West Brom's 'keeper looked – and must have felt – safe as houses. But the moment the ball was out of his possession, Kenny was in like a flash, to equalise.

Paisley made another point about the Scottish striker – 'he doesn't waste his time trying to get the ball in the air when he knows it's not on – he's looking to see where the ball will go next, and he's moving away to meet it'. Paisley described Dalglish as 'the coolest striker I've seen; some of his goals are fashioned almost clinically … for instance the one which won the European Cup final against Bruges in 1978. Graeme Souness showed great perception in putting the ball through, yet Kenny was ready and waiting for just such a pass. He was ready to react when the ball came, and he had already sized up the goalkeeper's likely reaction, as well'. In fact, as the 'keeper began to make his own move, Dalglish was looking beyond him, noting that there was a gap; and the Scot picked his spot with deadly accuracy as he delivered the chip over the 'keeper from a considerable angle.

In time, Bob Paisley was followed as manager by Joe Fagan, and when Joe decided to call it a day, it was Dalglish who got the nod from the Liverpool directors. Paisley then was said to be ready, willing and able to offer his advice – the voice of experience – should Kenny Dalglish require it. There did come a time when, according to one newspaper, it seemed as if Paisley and the player he had signed had lost the ability to communicate with each other. That was how it came out, at any rate, after Paisley had given an interview to a national newspaper. The inference was that Kenny didn't confide in Paisley any more, and there was no doubt that at the time the story broke it caused a great deal of embarrassment for two men who had given Liverpool Football Club sterling service. So much so, that Bob felt called upon to clear the air and make his peace with Dalglish. My own reading of the situation was that, as sometimes happened, what Bob had said during the interview might not have come out quite as he had intended it to do. One of those times when, for want of a better phrase, what he said required some interpreting as to what he actually meant. At any rate, harmony was restored, and when Bob retired from the club (by which time he was a director) he told me that the first person to ring him had been Dalglish – a nice touch, and one which most certainly was appreciated. From my own experience with Kenny, I know that he was not one for seeking out the media … and neither was Bob Paisley.

Once, with a wry smile on his face, Bob recalled what sometimes happened when the Sunday papers arrived in the Paisley household, and the previous day's game was under scrutiny. 'My wife, Jessie, used to say to me, "You didn't say that, did you?" Well, I had to admit that I hadn't meant to say that … it looks so different when it comes out in black and white'. He was right, of course – just as he was right when he offered the opinion that at Liverpool nobody had ever been considered more important than the club. 'It's never been allowed … the club has always been bigger than the individual. No one player has been allowed to come in and rule the roost'. He was right again, there – and very few players did try to show that they were the king-pins. Certainly neither Keegan nor Dalglish ever gave the impression of thinking they were the men who made Liverpool tick. Neither did Ian Rush.

When Paisley died, players and former players were among a host of football people who attended the chuch service which, at the family's request, had been restricted for reasons of privacy. Nevertheless, there were some 300 people there to pay their respects. Paisley himself wouldn't have wanted much fuss, of course – he was always like that. He would have appreciated, however, what one former managerial rival had to say about him – Tommy Docherty, whose Manchester United team destroyed Liverpool's dream of a unique treble in 1977. The Doc. had this to say about Bob: 'He was the best of the lot – look at his record. I think what I remember most about him is his humility. At the end of the 1977 final he was disappointed … but there was a nice little smile, and a handshake. He said, "Well done, Tom. I'm pleased for you". Not like so many today. He was a lovely man'.

Thus spoke Tommy Docherty, a man who had a nice line in pungent quips. Paisley, too, was a man with a lively sense of humour … how many managers would have in their office a clock that went backwards? – Whenever a visitor remarked on this seemingly odd piece of office furniture, Paisley would begin to chuckle – and then he would explain, as he informed his listeners just why the clock that went backwards occupied such a prominent spot. It seemed that whenever he had a player in, to discuss a problem or make a point, at the end of their chat Bob would point to the clock and say: 'There's one thing you can't do in football, son – and that's turn back the clock'.

It was a dictum which many of the men who played for Liverpool – and for Bob Paisley – would fervently echo, as the time arrived for them to walk out of the door at Anfield. Kevin Keegan, Kenny Dalglish, Ian Rush…

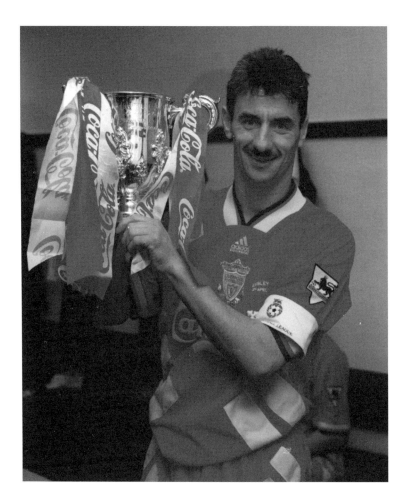

Ian Rush pictured after the Coca-Cola League Cup triumph in 1995. Since his arrival at Anfield in 1980, he has been one of Liverpool's most prolific scorers.

CHAPTER 9

The Rush Job

SOMEHOW, it seemed appropriate that around the time Bob Paisley died, Ian Rush announced that he would be leaving Liverpool. He had been a Paisley signing, back in April, 1980, and – after a few, pungent words from his manager – he had become one of the most prolific marksmen of all time in British football. With the death of Paisley and the impending departure of the man his team-mates called Rushy, it was the end of an era. Typically, Rush had not shouted the odds … he had asked to be allowed to leave before the March transfer deadline, but had been persuaded to stay on and see out season 1995-96. Liverpool were going for the championship and the F.A. Cup, at that stage of the campaign, and they didn't want to lose him, even if they could no longer guarantee him a place in the starting line-up. Rushy declared that he still felt he had another couple of years in him, even though he was 34; but he bowed to the club's request, and Liverpool said that at the end of the season, they would give him a free transfer. For his part, Rush said that he wasn't going to start a slanging match… 'Liverpool have been brilliant to me'. Bob Paisley would have approved of that sentiment.

Rush was leaving as a record-breaker in almost every respect – at the time it was revealed that he would be leaving (it was then the end of February) he had totalled 345 goals in 649 appearances, and just about the only thing he wouldn't be able to do was to break the 245 League-goal record of Roger Hunt. Rushy had managed 228, and he was running out of games. He was realistic enough to accept the fact that Robbie Fowler and Stan Collymore were forging a striking partnership, just as he had done alongside Kenny Dalglish.

At first, the up-and-coming Fowler had profited from the experience of the Welsh international, while Collymore – British football's costliest player, at £8.5 million – was being labelled a misfit, even as (after some four months at the club) he was expressing his unhappiness at the way things were going, and indicating that there might even be a parting of the ways. Liverpool, typically, were having none of this, and they swiftly hauled Stan the Man in and ensured that a statement from him put matters in perspective. Collymore declared that he wanted to carry on playing for Liverpool, and within a short space of time he was scoring goals and making quite a few for Fowler. As Ian Rush well knew, there was an old football saying that strikers hunt in pairs, and now the pairing was Fowler and Collymore.

Rushy was still bowing out as a hero – when he went on as substitute he was greeted with rapturous applause by the Anfield faithful – but when he looked back on his career, he could truthfully say that the dividing line between success and failure was slim, indeed. Collymore could probably say the same. So let us go back 16 years, to the time when the young Ian Rush was making his mark with Chester, down at Sealand Road. It was Cliff Sear, then the youth-development officer at Chester, who had kept tabs on the Welsh youngster as he played in schoolboy games and rattled in the goals as he represented Flintshire. Sear was to recall: 'I could not put him out of my mind'. As a one-time full-back who had totalled 250 appearances for Manchester City, Sear knew a scoring centre-forward when he saw one, and in Ian Rush he saw genuine potential. Rushy had never been one for making much noise – like Bob Paisley, he preferred to let his deeds do the talking for him, and when he went to Chester he was, according to Cliff Sear, 'very, very shy'. Sear said that the club used to provide a lunch of steak pie and chips… 'and Ian loved it'.

However, the day dawned when it was apparent that other, bigger clubs had taken notice of young Rush, who was still required to sign schoolboy forms. Sear spoke of driving to the Rush home in Flint – he described it as 'the longest journey of my life'. Sear was worried: would the lad opt for one of the bigger clubs? – But Rushy felt that Chester would be right for him, and so he signed. He became a first-teamer, and scored 14 goals in 33 Third Division outings. So Chester came under some pressure to capitalise on the youngster.

As he told me later, Ian had started out as an Everton fan; he also had a spell in an oxygen tent, when he fell victim to meningitis. 'The weight rolled off me then, and I never put it back on', he said. Cliff Sear and his manager at Chester, Alan Oakes, had been team-mates at Manchester City and, naturally, when the talk was of Rush being transferred, the Maine Road club was put on the alert. City watched him – and decided he wasn't quite ready for the big-time. Thus it was that Liverpool stepped in, and a £300,000 deal was agreed. Yet as time went by, it began to appear as if, for once, Bob Paisley and his backroom staff had failed to back a winner. Rush was given the chance to show what he could do, at first-team level, and he didn't manage a single goal in seven League games, the Milk Cup-final replay against West Ham, and the first leg of a European Cup semi-final against Bayern Munich. True enough, he had pace; but he wasn't scoring goals.

When he talked to Bob Paisley about the situation, the Liverpool manager gave him some succinct advice – in effect, he told Rushy to prove himself by starting to get his name on the scoresheet. Bob told me: 'I felt that he was making passes to others, instead of trying to stick the ball away himself. Sometimes this happens with young players when they get into the first team – they're a little bit afraid of trying something themselves, so they pass the ball to a team-mate'. That seemed to be the case, Paisley felt, with the Welsh lad – he wasn't being selfish enough. Those words from Bob Paisley must have gone home, however, because during the following season Rush the marksman really came out of his shell, as he totalled 48 games and struck 30 goals. His first in the League came on October 10, 1981, when he scored twice against Leeds United; and when he scored his first derby-game goal against Everton, it was to be the start of a haul which saw him break the legendary Dixie Dean's record.

I can look back now to the time he signed for Liverpool, and I quizzed Alan Oakes about Ian Rush. Oakes didn't hesitate to tell me then: 'Ian can go all the way to the top – I'm convinced of that'. And go to the top Rushy did, with Liverpool and with Wales … for whom he broke more records. In time, as Bob Paisley had done, Rush was to travel to London, the destination being Buckingham Palace, where he received the MBE. And football people generally reckoned he had earned it.

As the editor of Liverpool's match-day programme, I talked to virtually all the big-name players who passed through the portals at Anfield, and Rush was no exception. I found him to be modest, quietly-spoken and always co-operative. He might have been born across the border in Wales, but he spoke with the distinctive Scouse accent and, as Cliff Sear said, 'Ian the person hasn't changed one iota … he came from a good family background (he was one of a family of ten), and his feet have always been firmly on the floor'. When he took a testimonial match, with Glasgow Celtic providing the opposition, fans from around Britain – and abroad – flocked to Anfield to pay their tribute, and Rushy himself was almost overwhelmed by it all. He described it as one of the most emotional occasions of his life. During his final season with Liverpool, while I was on holiday near Cardiff, the Welsh-international team were staying in the same hotel as myself, and – as usual – Rushy was ready to oblige by signing his autograph. He also posed without demur for two ladies who wanted to have their photographs taken with him, as they held up a red jersey.

Cliff Sear reckoned that Rushy 'was given a gift to score goals; but with it went the hunger to succeed. It seems a long time since he sat down to steak pie and chips at Chester, but he remains the same, unassuming player, despite his medals and his world fame'. I wouldn't argue with that assessment of a footballer who graced the red shirt of club and country, and who broke so many records along the way. For instance, he overhauled the F.A. Cup scoring record of another master-marksman, Denis Law, when he clocked up goal No. 42 in a 7-0 win against Rochdale. At that time he was Liverpool's skipper, and he had just been awarded the MBE in the New Year's honours list. Not surprisingly, when Rushy struck that historic F.A. Cup goal, team-mates mobbed him and the Kop went wild. And yet … it was just one record in a lengthy list of records. For instance, his haul of goals in derby games against Everton – and these include an F.A. Cup final at Wembley. He became a record marksman with Wales, too; and when it came to rattling in hat-tricks, few could do it better. Ask Notts. County, who became his first hat-trick victims, in January, 1982. Games and goals? – They certainly added up, during the Liverpool career of Ian Rush … who, remember, in fact managed to have TWO careers with the Anfield club, because he left for Italy and then returned. Just as I had expected he would.

He even managed a hat-trick (against Pescara) during his spell with Juventus, though his Italian experience was not generally regarded as being among the most successful spells of his glittering career. The Rush haul of hat-tricks began when he was still playing schoolboy football – three goals for Wales against the Republic of Ireland lads. Once he had started to hit the target regularly for Liverpool, the goals flowed there, as well … that first hat-trick against Notts. County and then, in the following season, four goals against Everton, hat-tricks against Coventry City and poor old Notts. County again. During season 1983-84, Rush improved even upon that tally, as he lashed in five goals against hapless Luton Town, four against Coventry City and three against Aston Villa.

Season 1986-87 saw Rush adding to his tally of League hat-tricks with three goals against Leicester City, while in the final of the Screen Sport Super-Cup it was Everton who felt the impact of his markmanship. The F.A. Cup, the European Cup, the League Cup (which, of course, has gone under various names) all came into the picture as Rushy scored hat-tricks. In the sixth round of the F.A. Cup at Oakwell, during season 1984-85, Rush hit Barnsley with three goals, and his next F.A. Cup victims were Swansea City, during season 1989-90. The European Cup? – It was Benfica who suffered from a Rush hat-trick, in season 1984-85, while in season 1990-91 Crewe Alexandra wilted as Rush scored three times in what was then the Rumbelows League cup.

In November, 1994, it was Blackburn Rovers (and his old team-mate, Kenny Dalglish) who were left stunned as Rushy – making his 600th appearance for Liverpool – hit three goals to snuff out the Rovers' visions of appearing in the Coca-Cola Cup final. Mention of the hat-trick against Crewe brings a reminder that Rush had several other reasons to celebrate, during that campaign – he clocked up his 200th goal in the League, hit the 300th goal of his career, and clocked up his 500th appearance when he played for Liverpool against Norwich City at Carrow Road (Bob Paisley was there to see it). His hat-trick against Crewe (the 15th of his career) also saw him take his overall tally of goals past the 250 mark, while the 300th goal of his career came in April, 1991, against Crystal Palace at Anfield. All these scoring feats were remarkable, by any standard –

and, of course, with them came winner's medals in just about every competition.

If Rushy's testimonial night was one of the most emotional occasions of his glittering career, so was the day he played his farewell match (the first time around) for Liverpool. That game was against Watford, on the eve of his departure for the land of the lire … and, naturally, it was Rush who turned out to be the match-winner. Liverpool were receiving more than £3 million as their consolation prize for losing Ian Rush, and before he left these shores I talked with him about his transfer to the Italian giants, Juventus. At the end of our conversation, I would have bet money that Rushy's stay in Italy would not be all that long – and it wasn't because I was doubting his ability to measure up to the demands of the game out there.

More than a few players have left these isles for the land of the lire … going back to the Gentle Giant, John Charles, to Jimmy Greaves, Joe Baker and Denis Law, to Gerry Hitchens, and – more recently – to players such as Ray Wilkins, Trevor Francis, Luther Blissett, Gordon Cowans, Paul Rideout, Graeme Souness. Some prospered more than others. My reason for thinking that Ian Rush wouldn't be staying long was, partly, that distinctive, Scouse accent of his – I just felt that he was a Liverpudlian Welshman at heart, and that the football alone wouldn't be sufficient. I simply couldn't see him settling into the environment out there, and when I asked him about the language problem, he told me that Tracy – the girl he married – was taking lessons in Italian, while 'I've got a phrase book'.

It was Monday, May 4, 1987, when Ian Rush played his farewell game, against Watford, and, of course, I made certain that the front page of the programme for that match featured the Welsh international – oddly enough, it showed him in action against an Everton defender, Dave Watson, whose own career had begun at Liverpool. As usual, I compiled the programme notes for Kenny Dalglish, and this is what he had to say about the player who had been his team-mate: 'Ian Rush has been one of the greatest players ever to wear a Liverpool jersey, and we have been privileged that he has served us so well and contributed so much as a team man. We're sorry to see him go – but I can tell him that he'll always be welcome to come back and beat Dixie Dean's record!' Which, in fact, Rushy did. Naturally, I had talked to Ian himself about his career, and he admitted that he had been 'a bit wary about the reaction to my impending move to Italy'.

It had been known since the start of the season that Liverpool would be losing him to Juventus, and Rushy confessed: 'I didn't know how the fans would take it. But after the Charity Shield game against Everton (in the August) when they started shouting my name, I really wanted to do well for them. They've been great to me. I'm also thankful that the club gave me my big chance by signing me from Chester, and I like to think I've repaid Liverpool's faith'. Rush then referred to the club he had supported as a kid – 'my outstanding memories are of two games against Everton. First, when we beat them in the F.A. Cup final and did the double by winning the League title. I don't think many other clubs will achieve that – and the fact that we won the Cup by beating Everton made it something special again. Everything was rolled into one, in that game. Then came my final derby game, when I equalled Dixie Dean's scoring record'. Rushy signed off by saying: 'This season has had its disappointments for us, but I reckon I've still been lucky, because I've had a lot more good times than bad. And that means I'll take with me plenty of happy memories'. Indeed, he did.

The last goal Ian Rush had scored for Chester had come during a home game against Colchester United on April 12, 1980 – after having failed to find the net in five previous matches, he struck twice, to demolish Colchester's hopes of promotion. His goals meant that Chester won, 2-1 – and he had been a winner ever since. Yes, even though at the age of six he had been struck down with meningitis … because, after three weeks in an oxygen tent he made a complete recovery, to win that battle, as well. He could recall that a team-mate had claimed an F.A. Cup goal which, Rushy reckoned, should have been his – otherwise he would have overtaken Denis Law's record earlier. He could reflect upon the words of Bob Paisley, when he was striving to find top form at Liverpool – and the words of Alan Oakes, his former boss at Chester … 'possibly Ian will not have to become impatient to get into Liverpool's first team too quickly; but time is on his side and, in the end, I think he will be a very good player for Liverpool. I reckon he can go all the way to the top'. Rushy could recall, also, the first League match he ever saw – Spurs versus Liverpool, at White Hart Lane … and his first medal after joining Liverpool: this arrived when he was on the winning side in the 1981 League Cup-final replay against West Ham.

Rushy could go back to his days as an 11-year-old stripling … when he hit 72 goals as Deeside Primary Schools won all their 33 matches; he could go back to season 1982-83 with Liverpool, when his four goals against Everton in a Goodison Park derby game equalled a record which had stood for 47 years; and he could recall what Barnsley defender Paul Futcher had said about him, after that FA Cup hat-trick… 'Short of getting a double-barrelled shotgun and blowing his head off, I don't think he can be stopped'. His one-time Welsh-team manager, Mike England, described him as 'one of the most exciting forwards around', while former England manager Bobby Robson termed him 'a match-winning player … he has speed off the mark and composure in front of goal. He has to play in areas where there is little time or space, because of tight marking'.

When Rush left Liverpool, Kenny Dalglish replaced him with another marksman, John Aldridge, who quickly became a favourite with the fans as he plundered goals in the style of his predecessor. When Rush returned to Liverpool, at a cost of some £2.8 million, after chief executive Peter Robinson had been tipped off that a reverse transfer could be on the cards, the fans wondered who would make way for whom. In the end, it was Rush who regained the No.1 spot, Aldo who moved on, to Real Sociedad – after scoring from the spot in a 9-0 demolition job Liverpool did on Crystal Palace. Rush reigned supreme once again, until the arrival of Graeme Souness as team boss – when, towards the end of the Souness era, the Welsh star found himself not only being named as captain, but being dropped and substituted.

When Rushy returned to Liverpool and we discussed his stay with Juventus, he told me: 'I don't regret having gone to Italy … it was a good career move for me. But now that I'm back, I hope to stay at Liverpool for the rest of my top-class career'. In his final derby game before going to Italy, he equalled Dixie Dean's 19-goal, derby-game record; and he answered the invitation by Kenny Dalglish to overhaul that record when he went on to make it 23 goals in two dozen derby games. Remarkably, not one of these had come from the penalty spot. By 1995 he had totalled 25 goals in games against Everton … and there was that astonishing, 4-4 F.A. Cup-replay draw against Everton at Goodison Park which was the signal for Dalglish himself to stun Soccer by announcing: 'I quit'. And so Graeme Souness – 'this fellow', as Bob Paisley said to me – came in as manager.

By then, Paisley was not in the best of health, and as time went by his health deteriorated further. Meanwhile, Souness signed and sold players as he brought about what Peter Robinson was to term 'a revolution' at Anfield. Rush was to become one of the victims, albeit temporarily. When Paisley recalled how the young Rush had gone to see him, early in his Liverpool career, he said: 'He was struggling … he was probably too unselfish at the time. That's often the case with a young player, particularly one coming into a successful side. He tended to look for others and lay the ball off when he could have had a go himself. I told him to be a bit more selfish, and it wasn't long before the penny dropped'. Rush struck his first-ever goal for Liverpool when he went on as a substitute against Oulu Palloseura in a European match on September 30, 1981; and 10 days later came that first, First Division goal, against Leeds United.

While with Juventus, he scored 14 goals, and though his return to Liverpool initally wasn't easy, partly because he had been weakened by illness, he hit the scoring trail once more, with Roger Hunt declaring: 'It looks to me as if he is now back to the form he showed before he went to Italy. I think he's the best in the modern game, and his record proves it. The game has changed a lot since my day – it's quickened up and tightened up. There was more attacking when I played, and more chances. It's all the more credit to him that he's got his goals in this era'. He did equal Hunt's overall, 286-goal feat with a goal in the Coca-

Cola Cup replay against Chesterfield – that was in the Souness era, and there were a couple of occasions when Rushy and his boss didn't see eye to eye. There was also a time when the Welsh international said his piece, for once, about Liverpool Football Club.

Having been dropped for the first time in his career, before a game at Hillsborough, he rapped: 'It would have been better if the manager had choen to speak to me first' (Rushy had learned he was out, from the media, only an hour before the kick-off). He declared: 'I'm upset about it, but I'll be fighting to get back'. He was then 31, and it was March, 1993. Twelve months on, he was looking back at two more matches which had left him feeling less than happy – a demotion to substitute as Liverpool lost 3-1 against Sheffield Wednesday, and being replaced by Mark Walters near the end of a game at Bramall Lane.

Rush then was Liverpool's skipper, and it was recorded that he 'spent the last eight minutes with arms folded, pointedly standing several feet from the bench'. He admitted: 'It always hurts when you're the one taken off. I don't know why it was me – that's up to the manager. As to whether we talk about it later, that's between him and me'. There came a day – the last day of season 1993-94 – when Rushy scored twice in a 6-2 mauling of Spurs … that day, also, Souness (not for the first time) was the subject of great speculation about his job. On the radio, when asked about this, Rush sidestepped cleverly, and when pushed to say if he wanted Souness to stay or go, he declared that his own job was to keep on doing his best for Liverpool. At one stage, however, he did come out and say it was time Liverpool spoke up and said if their manager was staying or going, to clear the air for everyone's sake. And he also defended his manager when Souness was under severe pressure from the media.

In the end, what was termed 'people power' decided Souness's fate, after an F.A. Cup reverse at Anfield, though Souness himself made the decision to go. Rush remained at Anfield, and as young Robbie Fowler graduated to first-team football, Leeds United 'keeper John Lukic offered the opinion that Rush had 'learned his trade and picked up the tricks from playing alongside Kenny Dalglish … now Fowler is learning in the same way from Rushy'. When Rush staged his testimonial match, the gate was close on 26,000 and record receipts were estimated at quarter of a million pounds gross. Rush, his wife, Tracy, and their sons, Daniel and Jonathan, were there to savour the occasion – one which, as Rushy confessed, made him feel a touch nervous. By then, he had totalled 601 games for Liverpool, topped the 330-goal mark, as well as the all-time record for Wales (with 28 international goals); and, at the age of 33, he remained first choice for club and country. Season 1995-96 was to be the one which determined his future plans, as he took the decision to part company with the club he had joined almost 16 years earlier. Manager Roy Evans – like Rush, a Paisley protége

– talked it through with the player, then said: 'He is staying until the end of the season. He wants to help us achieve something, and we are delighted with his attitude'. At one stage during the previous season or two, there had been talk of a move to Manchester City – or even Everton. Now … who could tell?

Rush himself reflected: 'I believe I have another two years left in me, and I just want to play. The way it's going, I have to look to my future, and so have Liverpool. They have just been brilliant to me, right through the years, but I have reluctantly decided it's time to move on. It's going to be a massive wrench'. He had clearly accepted that there was going to be no swift reinstatement as a first-team regular, in the face of the competition from Fowler and Collymore. And, ever the realist, he had demonstrated also his acceptance of something Bob Paisley used to tell other players… 'There's one thing you can't do, in football – and that's turn back the clock!'

Alan Hansen, pictured carrying the Charity Shield won in 1989. The Scottish defender captained Liverpool to the Double in the 1985/86 season, and made over 450 appearances for Liverpool before injury cut his career short.

CHAPTER 10

Picking Winners

THE chairman of a Premiership club said to me one day: 'I can't half pick 'em!' He was referring to the managers he had hired – and fired – and he was smiling somewhat wryly, as he delivered this verdict. As a manager who didn't want the job, Bob Paisley could have said something similar… 'I can't half pick 'em!' … this, when it came to delivering the verdict about the players he signed for Liverpool. And in his case, he could have been forgiven had he been smiling broadly; because, as a judge of footballing talent, he was almost in a class of his own. Paisley made very few mistakes, if any, when he forked out Liverpool's money on reinforcements.

You could start at the back, with Bruce Grobbelaar, go along the back-four line, with Phil Neal, Mark Lawrenson, Alan Hansen and Alan Kennedy. Take the midfield, and you had players such as Terry McDermott and Graeme Souness; and up front there was Kenny Dalglish to replace Kevin Keegan, with Ian Rush as the partner for King Kenny. Other players arrived at Anfield during the Paisley era, while the home-grown crop included Ian Callaghan, Jimmy Case, David Fairclough, Steve Heighway, Brian Hall, Sammy Lee and Phil Thompson. Steve Nicol was one of Paisley's best buys; David Johnson – a Merseysider who had kicked off with Everton – arrived from Ipswich Town; while Ronnie Whelan came from Dublin and Craig Johnston hailed from Johannesburg, though he was signed from Middlesbrough. All in all, that little lot constituted more than a team and a half … and in their various ways, they did Bob Paisley and Liverpool Football Club proud.

Paisley, I have no doubt, would have been saddened even to think that Bruce Grobbelaar would end up being accused of 'throwing' matches – this extrovert 'keeper arrived at Anfield because, as Grobbelaar himself told me, Liverpool's manager was persistent enough to travel to Canada to watch him, and to cope with the business of obtaining a work permit. Paisley was also strong enough to tell Grobbelaar when to cut out the clowning – such as doing handstands out on the pitch while the game was still in progress … even if it was to celebrate a Liverpool goal. The story of Grobbelaar's arrival at Liverpool was told to me by Tom Saunders, who in his time followed Paisley as a man who filled almost every possible role at Anfield … youth-development officer, assessor of the opposition, talent-spotter, elder statesman and, probably, father-confessor, at times, as well.

Tom was deputed to travel to Fratton Park to check on a Portsmouth player. When he got there, his attention was drawn to the opposition's goalkeeper – Grobbelaar, who was playing for Crewe Alexandra. Pompey needed two points to claim a promotion place, Grobbelaar stopped almost everything they could throw at him. The match ended 1-1, and when Saunders returned to Liverpool he told Paisley about the 'keeper. So Bob went with Tom to watch Crewe in mid-week, and the 'keeper impressed even during the pre-match kickabout. 'What stood out was his handling of the ball and his general athleticism', Tom told me. However, Grobbelaar was registered with Vancouver Whitecaps, so the next move was up to Liverpool. Paisley and Saunders flew to watch Grobbelaar in action in Canada. Once again, the 'keeper impressed – and the fact that he had played at international level for Zimbabwe helped, when it came to overcoming work-permit problems.

Grobbelaar had been unable to get a work permit during a five-month spell with West Brom, and he had briefly been at Bournemouth, and on loan at Crewe. He told me, after he had joined Liverpool: 'Bob Paisley was the only manager interested enough to fly to Vancouver to see me there, and Liverpool were the only club which persisted in trying to solve the work-permit problem'. So, in March, 1981, he was signed by Liverpool for £250,000 … and by the start of the following season he was being pitched in at the deep end, because Ray Clemence had shocked Liverpool with the news that he was ready to leave.

His departure for Spurs, after more than 650 games for Liverpool, paved the way for the goalkeeper who was labelled by one writer as 'truly an enigma'. Grobbelaar, it was recorded, 'mixes brilliance with an adventurous streak which sometimes costs the team'. He was to win praise for some displays, be criticised for having had 'a rush of blood to the head' at other times; yet, overall, he won medals galore as he remained Liverpool's last line of defence and saw off more than one claimant to the goalkeeping crown at Anfield. For quite a while Alan Hansen was Liverpool's skipper, and he told me that Grobbelaar's great strengths were 'his reflexes and his agility'. Hansen also said: 'When he was under pressure, he shrugged it off, even though things were hard for him. He fought back well'.

Grobbelaar survived through the managerial careers of Paisley, Joe Fagan, Kenny Dalglish and Graeme Souness (although the 'keeper and Souness had more than one publicised difference of opinion). It was during the early stages of the Roy Evans era that Grobbelaar indicated his days at Anfield could be drawing to a close. He had declared: 'I want to play for Liverpool until I lose my smile … or until they put me out to grass'. And he summed up what it took to be a goalkeeper: 'You need to be a bit crazy and have a skin as thick as a turtle shell, because you'll always get flak'. Still, he said he would 'carry on taking all the stick they dish out, just so long as I can keep on enoying the good times'. They were about to disappear, as he and Liverpool failed to agree on a new deal, and so Grobbelaar made his exit. Not long after he had landed at Southampton he had to face up to 'the flak' – this time in the shape of newspaper allegations that he taken money for 'throwing' matches. The Grobbelaar affair ran on and on … it was on November 14, 1994, that he was charged by the Football Assocation with bringing the game into disrepute and accepting 'a consideration' for influencing results; and by the spring of 1996, he was still awaiting a verdict as to whether or not he had been found guilty, along with Hans Segers and John Fashanu. All three men had denied the allegations against them.

Phil Neal, to whom I have referred earlier, totalled 635 games and scored 60 goals for Liverpool; and alongside him was a player whom many judges rated as the finest all-rounder in the land – Mark Lawrenson, signed by Paisley from Brighton for £900,000 in August, 1981. Elegant and composed, like his partner, Alan Hansen, at the heart of the defence, Lawrenson was a key player in the team which did the double in season 1985-86, and although he played well over 250 games for Liverpool, he would surely have totalled many more but for the injury which curtailed his top-class career … just as it did for Hansen, who nevertheless managed to repay the £100,000 transfer fee by playing more than 450 senior games. It was Hansen who skippered Liverpool to the double.

Then, of course, there was the man the fans loved to call Barney Rubble (he of the Flintstones fame)… Alan Kennedy; and bracketed with Kennedy must be the name of Steve Nicol. While Kennedy – whose goal won the European Cup for Liverpool in 1981 – was an out-and-out left-back who could go on a storming run, Nicol was Mr. Versatile himself; he could play in either of the full-back positions, in the middle of the defence, or on the right or left side of midfield. And when you weighed up Kennedy and Nicol, and the contribution they made to the cause of Liverpool Football Club, you still hadn't taken into account a Welsh defender by the name of Joey Jones – he was not only the epitome of a Liverpool player … he was a dyed-in-the-wool Liverpool fan. Nicol, said Bob Paisley, was 'one for the future' when he arrived from Ayr United in October, 1981 – and how well he repaid Liverpool through more than a decade of service. Like Hansen and Jones, as well as Lawrenson, he figured in some of Liverpool's most triumphant seasons.

Then you had McDermott, Ray Kennedy, Case and Souness in midfield. McDermott, the Scouser who went to Wembley with Newcastle United, only to finish up on the wrong end of a 3-0 scoreline, as Liverpool went home with the F.A. Cup. Alan Kennedy, too, was like McDermott that day – he wore Newcastle's colours, and finished feeling choked with disappointment. But both players were to make up for that disastrous afternoon, during their time at Anfield. As for Case and Souness, they could both play football a man's way.

Not that Ray Kennedy was a faintheart, either … he was a big lad and well able to take care of hmself. He had been Bill Shankly's final signing, whereas Souness was a Paisley buy, and he cost what was then a club-record fee of £352,000 when he moved from Middlesbrough in January, 1978. Not long before, he had played at Anfield as a member of Boro's team, and his signing was to have a genuine impact upon the results Liverpool managed to achieve. During his seven seasons at Anfield he totalled more than 350 appearances and scored 56 goals, and when he left Liverpool for Sampdoria, he brought the Anfield club £650,000. Souness told me on his arrival that just because he had cost such a big fee he didn't expect automatic entry to the first team – 'I know I've got to earn my place', he said. But by the end of his first season, in the spring of 1978, he was not only a regular … he was providing the astute pass for Kenny Dalglish to chip the Bruges goalkeeper and ensure that the European Cup remained on the Anfield sideboard.

Souness possessed just about all the attributes required for a top-class midfielder: he could beat a man by sheer skill – in fact, some of his football had a silky touch about it; on the other hand, he could be hard as nails when the going got rough; and he could win heading duels, while he packed a fierce shot. His game, it was said, was about delicate ball play and accurate distribution, 'sprinkled with a touch of arrogance'. He wanted to be a winner every time out, and he demanded the same approach from his team-mates – just as he demanded it from the players who were there during his time as manager of Liverpool. He could rub people the wrong way, and he could lose his rag at times; but while he might not have been idolised as Kenny Dalglish was, he was always respected, even admired, for the qualities he brought to the team game at Liverpool. Bob Paisley may have bowed out as manager by 1984, but Souness was still strutting his stuff – scoring the winner against Everton in the Milk Cup-final replay, striking the ball home from the penalty spot as Liverpool won the European Cup final in a shoot-out against AS Roma in Rome.

If Terry McDermott was not quite cast in the Souness mould, another midfield man signed during the Paisley era wasn't far behind the controversial Scot – Ronnie Whelan. McDermott's forte was to make penetrating runs which got him into scoring positions; Whelan was more the Souness type.

'Terry Mac' had joined Bury as an apprentice, then moved up the Soccer scale to Newcastle United. However, this Scouser born in Kirkby (Phil Thompson came from there, too) did sufficient in the 1974 F.A. Cup final to make Liverpool think of taking him back to his native Merseyside, and he arrived at Anfield in the November after the Wembley final. At first, he had a bit of a battle to make the breakthrough, and many people saw him as little more than an othodox wing-half; but gradually, he began to make his presence felt, and by the time the 1977 European Cup final came round he was a recognised part of the Liverpool unit – indeed, he was a marksman against Borussia Moenchengladbach. In fact, McDermott totalled more than 300 senior games for Liverpool and scored 75 goals. In 1980 he received the accolade as he was voted Footballer of the Year; and then, in September, 1982, he returned to Newcastle United, to help Kevin Keegan and his team-mates achieve promotion.

It was at the start of the 1980's that Ronnie Whelan, like Ian Rush, began to make his name at Liverpool – originally, as Whelan himself told me, he had been rated a certainty to end up at Manchester United, because Old Trafford was his destination during school holidays. But in the end he landed at Liverpool, and this son of a Republic of Ireland international showed that he could display skill and strength, as he became a first-team regular. Like Rush and Souness, he captained Liverpool, totalled well over 200 games and more than 50 goals, and – after having scored on his League debut, like Dalglish – he went on to claim a winner's medal in the League, the European Cup and the F.A. Cup, while in the League-Milk Cup final he was on the mark twice as Liverpool despatched Spurs at Wembley, and a year later he was the match-winner there against Manchester United in the same competition. Once again, it was a case of Whelan playing under new management (Kenny Dalglish) when he was a member of the double-winning side in season 1985-86. But he had arrived during the Paisley era.

David Johnson and Craig Johnston came in, respectively, during the middle and towards the end of the Paisley era ... the former arrived as a £200,000 signing from Ipswich, though he had begun his career with Everton – indeed, he had carved out a reputation as a hat-trick man; as for Johnston, he cost £575,000 when he left Middlesbrough in April, 1981.

It really took David Johnson a few seasons to force his way into the first team on a regular basis, but in season 1978-79 he had become established, and the next term saw him finishing as Liverpool's leading scorer, with 21 League goals in 37 outings, plus half a dozen in Cup matches. He was in Liverpool's losing, 1977 F.A. Cup-final side, figured in their 1981, victorious European Cup-winning team ... than Ian Rush started to bang in the goals, and Johnson's career slowly began to fade at Anfield. In 1982 he returned to his first senior club, Everton, and Liverpool recouped £100,000. Meanwhile, Craig Johnston – who had arrived at Middlesbrough via a couple of Australian clubs, Lake McQuarrie and Sydney City – proved himself to be an immensely strong player whose stamina matched that of Kevin Keegan. In many ways, his style of play reminded you of Keegan, although he didn't possess the same flair for finding the net. He did score the goal which gave Liverpool the lead in the 1986 F.A. Cup final against Everton, and he totalled close on 200 senior appearances during the five seasons which ended with Liverpool doing the double.

When you consider the number of players who joined Liverpool during the Paisley era, it can be seen that altogether they did not represent a fortune, when compared with the club's outlay of £8.5 million on one of its current stars. Of course, prices then were not what they have become since Soccer became affluent in the Sky-dominated era; but when you talk about value for money, Paisley most certainly ensured that Liverpool didn't miss out. For something like £3 million in total, Liverpool got virtually a team of players, and every single one of them contributed considerably to the club's dazzling success under Bob Paisley. Add to this the fact that home-produced footballers were neither neglected nor ignored, and the benefits can be seen to have been enormous. True, not every home-grown player was down to Paisley – some arrived during the Shankly period – but Callaghan, Case, Fairclough, Hall, Heighway, Lee and Phil Thompson did their whack for Paisley. Thompson, especially, graced the Anfield scene through a dozen seasons, while Cally's career lasted through the best part of 20 years. Come to that, Tommy Smith played through 15 seasons, and a Shankly signing – John Toshack – played his part while Paisley was at the helm. Cally totalled a record-breaking, 850 games, Thompson more than 460, and Smith more than 630.

They certainly built 'em to last, in those days – at Liverpool, more than most, as both Emlyn Hughes and Chris Lawler, to name two more stalwarts, demonstrated. Like Thompson, Hughes captained club and country, stayed at Liverpool for 13 seasons – which meant from season 1966-67 to season 1978-79 – during which he played 657 games. Lawler? – His Anfield career had begun in season 1962-63, and not until season 1975-76 had arrived did he give up, as he managed just a single game – though that one was in European competition. In 546 appearances overall he hit 61 goals, and if his career was drawing to its close by the time Bob Paisley took up the reins, he still got in a handful of games after Shankly had gone. All in all, Paisley bought supremely well, utilised the talent at his command to its full potential, and in the process moulded teams which won trophies galore … the personnel changed with the passing years, but the story of singular success never really altered.

CHAPTER 11

A Spoke in the Wheel

IN SHANKLY'S day, the major opposition came from Harry Catterick's Everton and Don Revie's Leeds United; in Paisley's day, if there was one manager who could claim, however remotely, to have had the Indian sign on Liverpool, it was the self-styled 'Old Big 'Ead' himself, Brian Clough. Long before Clough was arousing the ire of Liverpool supporters by his criticisms of them over the Hillsborough tragedy. he was putting into words what so many people privately acknowledged, when he declared: 'He's broken this silly myth that nice guys don't win anything. He's one of the nicest guys you could meet in any industry or any walk of life – and he is a winner'. Clough, of course, was referring to Bob Paisley, whom he succeeded as Manager of the Year in 1978.

Such a handsome compliment didn't mean, however, that Brian Clough wouldn't do his level best to ensure that his Nottingham Forest side put one across Paisley's team, and it was during the late 1970's that Forest put more than one spoke in Liverpool's seemingly unstoppable wheels. Liverpool had achieved a magnificent double of League championship and European Cup in season 1976-77, missing out narrowly on what would have been a unique treble, as Manchester United lifted the F.A. Cup. Twelve months later, the championship trophy was being lifted by Brian Clough's team, as Nottingham Forest finished ahead of the pack, on 64 points. It was a season when Forest also pipped Liverpool for another trophy … the League Cup, though it needed a replay and a controversial goal to do the trick.

Liverpool had Kenny Dalglish in their ranks when they kicked off at Ayresome Park, and his debut goal earned a point against Middlesbrough. Liverpool then reeled off five straight wins, including a 2-0 success in the League Cup-tie against Chelsea. Their victims in the League were Newcastle United, West Brom, Birmingham City and Coventry City, and as Liverpool rattled in eight goals against the four clubs, they didn't concede even one. Ipswich held them to a 1-1 draw at Portman Road, Derby County lost 1-0 at Anfield, then Manchester United – at Old Trafford – became the first to conquer Paisley's team, winning 2-0. Liverpool then embarked upon another run … 0-0 at Highbury, 2-0 in the Anfield League game against Chelsea, 2-1 away against Leeds United and, in the European Cup, 5-1 at home against Dynamo Dresden.

It was 0-0 in the Anfield derby game against Everton, 2-0 against Derby County in the League Cup-tie at Anfield, then – surprise, surprise – four defeats on the trot … 1-3 at Maine Road, 1-2 in the European Cup return, 1-2 at home against Aston Villa and 0-2 against Queen's Park Rangers at Loftus Road. It was what became known as the Liverpool wobble, though the rot was stopped with a 1-1 draw against Bristol City at Anfield and a similar scoreline in the away leg of the European Super-Cup against SV Hamburg. Liverpool showed they were no spent force as they hammered Leicester City 4-0 at Filbert Street, drew 2-2 with Coventry City in the League Cup-tie at Anfield, beat West Ham 2-0 and SV Hamburg 6-0 in the Super-Cup return, and lost only one game out of the next half-dozen, which took them to the turn of the year.

That defeat came at Norwich, by the odd goal in three, then after a 1-0 home win over Queen's Park Rangers, Liverpool put the Sky Blues of Coventry in their place by going to Highfield Road and winning the League Cup replay 2-0. The next outing was against Nottingham Forest, at the City Ground, and a hard-earned point with a 1-1 draw left Paisley and his players feeling happy. Wolves lost 1-0 at Anfield, Newcastle were beaten 2-0 at St. James's Park, to make it a League double over the Magpies, and the first game of the New Year brought Liverpool a 2-0 home victory in the return against Middlesbrough. However, when Liverpool went to Stamford Bridge for the third round of the F.A. Cup, they came a cropper – beaten 4-2. One doorway into Europe had been closed.

There were two tricky away fixtures next, as well – in the League at West Brom and in the League Cup at Wrexham, but Liverpool emerged as the victors each time, with Dalglish coming through as a hat-trick hero at Wrexham. Then Liverpool came unstuck with a 3-2 home defeat by Birmingham in the League and a 1-0 defeat at Coventry. Which brought them to the semi-final stage of the League Cup, and a confrontation with Arsenal. The first leg was at Anfield, and after 90 minutes Liverpool had to be satisfied with a narrow victory – 2-1 – as they looked ahead to the return match in a week's time. They went to Highbury, and they held out for a scoreless draw, so they had reached their goal … the final at Wembley. And in the League match immediately after the Arsenal duel they defeated Manchester United 3-1 at Anfield, to avenge that 2-0 result at Old Trafford.

By this time it was coming up to March, and Liverpool's opponents in the European Cup were the Eagles of Lisbon, Benfica, with the away leg first. Liverpool put up a tremendous performance in Lisbon's Stadium of Light to return with a 2-1 victory, thanks to goals from Jimmy Case and Emlyn Hughes; then they had to forget about Europe as they took on Chelsea, Derby County and Leeds United in the League. They lost the first two of those games, beat Leeds, and went into the European Cup return hoping to make it to the semi-finals … which they did, on the back of a 4-1 success, as the goals flowed from

Ian Callaghan, Kenny Dalglish, Terry McDermott and Phil Neal. By then – and it was mid-March, with the season's end still almost two months away – Liverpool had already played 45 matches (31 of them during the first half of the season) and, although they didn't know it, they were to face another 16 games before they could call it a day. After Benfica at Anfield, in fact, it was a case of switching venues to the place Liverpool's players had come to call Anfield South – Wembley; there to meet Nottingham Forest in the final of the League Cup. And it had to be admitted that Liverpool were going to Wembley as favourites. Forest, indeed, were said to be in a bit of a quandary, because they would have to make do without the vastly-experienced Peter Shilton in goal; instead, Brian Clough would be forced to throw in a youngster by the name of Chris Woods. The omens appeared to favour Liverpool, as they faced this virtually-untried last line of defence.

Brian Clough, of course, had his own, unique method of preparing his team for the big occasion – he was a master in the art of getting them relaxed, of sending them out in the right mood to do battle. And he made it clear that he had every confidence in the young Chris Woods and his ability to cope with everything that Liverpool could throw at him. His confidence turned out not to have been misplaced, either, because early in the game, as Liverpool tried to take control, when Dalglish broke through it was Woods who went down bravely to foil the Scot, and from that moment on, it seemed as if the entire Forest team had been given the signal to raise their game. Not that they threatened to over-run the opposition … Liverpool still contrived to be in control,but while they drove forward time and again, Forest stood firm, and no goals came. Even David Fairclough, who was sent on in the hope that he would achieve the breakthrough, couldn't produce a match-winner, and extra time came and went, with still not a goal in sight.

At the end, 100,000 people trooped away from Wembley stadium, knowing that if they wanted to see the return match, they must take their chances of getting into Old Trafford the following Wednesday night. I had been to the match at Wembley, and I was at Old Trafford for what might be termed the second half of this marathon final. It was to end in deep disappointment for Liverpool, as Forest scored the only goal. In their side, as at Wembley, were men who had played for Brian Clough elsewhere … John McGovern, John O'Hare; they also had Frank Clark (who was to manage Forest during the 1990's), Kenny Burns, Peter Withe, Tony Woodcock, the stocky Scottish winger, John Robertson, and a former Liverpool defender, Larry Lloyd. And at Old Trafford, they were awarded a penalty which Liverpool players claimed should never have been given … yet the referee's decision was final and, as ever, they had to accept it. Up strode Robertson, cool as a cucumber, and he despatched the spot-kick past

Ray Clemence. It was a blow from which Liverpool, for all their fighting spirit and commitment, could not recover. They had deserved better, they felt, from the encounter at Wembley, but now it just wasn't to be their night. And so Brian Clough and his players were the ones who enjoyed the occasion at Old Trafford, while Liverpool were left to rue the might-have-beens.

Like Liverpool, Forest were now going for a double – they had their hands round the League Cup, and they were after the championship trophy, as well. That was a trophy which Liverpool wanted to retain, just as they wanted to retain the European Cup. And the games were coming thick and fast … after Forest in the Cup final it was Wolves away (Liverpool won, 3-1), then the first leg of the European Cup semi-final … against the team they had defeated in the final in Rome almost a year earlier. Yes, Borussia Moenchengladbach barred the way once again, and this time Liverpool's fans wondered if the Germans would obtain their revenge. The first leg was in Germany, and 66,000 people flocked to the stadium to see who would emerge as the victors. It turned out to be Borussia, although the margin was slender enough – 2-1. However, it had taken a goal by David Johnson, only two minutes from full time, for Liverpool to be given the chance of a reprieve. It was a game in which Graeme Souness went on to replace Steve Heighway and in which Johnson had proved to be an inspired substitution as he replaced McDermott.

Liverpool faced three stiff fixtures before the second leg – away against Aston Villa and Everton, at home to Leicester City – and they lifted themselves to win all three matches. So they were still in contention for the championship, still ready to battle their way through to the final of the European Cup. Forest, too, were still on course for the League title – in fact, by the time the season was drawing to its close and each club had four games to go, Forest led the pack with 59 points and Liverpool were in fourth place, on 50 points. By then, the race was all but won, but in the meantime, Liverpool kept on pegging away. And when Borussia arrived at Anfield, the scene was set for a dramatic encounter, with the Germans resolved to cling on to their slim advantage. Inside the first 10 minutes, however, Liverpool fans were roaring as Kennedy struck, to make the score 2-2 on aggregate; then Dalglish made it 2-0 on the night, to put Liverpool ahead overall – and there were still 10 minutes to go to half-time. The 51,000 inside Anfield looked eagerly for more goals … but by the interval, it was still 2-0. Borussia had 45 minutes in which to stage a rescue act; Liverpool had 45 minutes in which to deliver a killer blow. And it was Liverpool who produced the goal that saw off their opponents, as Jimmy Case struck their third, just inside the hour. As they had been in Rome, Borussia were a beaten side and Liverpool were on their way … back to Wembley, where the final would be staged.

Their opponents there would be FC Bruges – the club which had given Liverpool such a scare in the 1976 final of the UEFA Cup – so, once again, nothing could be taken for granted. Liverpool remembered, all too vividly, as well, how they had fared against Forest at Wembley just a few weeks earlier … and how they had lost that League Cup-final replay at Old Trafford. But before the meeting with Bruges there remained seven League matches to be played, and in turn Liverpool drew away with Bristol City and at home against Ipswich Town, beat Norwich City and Arsenal at Anfield, won at West Ham and at home against Manchester City and, finally, drew (no score) at Anfield against Nottingham Forest. For the second time that season, it was a bitter-sweet experience for Bob Paisley and his players, because when Forest played that final League game, they had the championship in their grasp. For Brian Clough, the double had come up – League Cup and League title; for Liverpool, who were destined to finish second, it had become a matter of salvaging something from the last remaining match … the European Cup final.

The game itself was a contrast to the drama of what had gone before, when Liverpool had won the trophy in Rome. This final, against FC Bruges, was not one filled with goals, and in many respects it was somewhat dour, a kind of low-key affair, even though there were 92,000 partisan fans in the stadium. The first half remained scoreless, and the longer the game went the more people began to think about extra time. This time out, Daivd Fairclough had been in Liverpool's starting line-up, while Steve Heighway had been sitting it out on the bench; but, as the game progressed, Paisley decided that Heighway should get into the action and so he replaced Case. However, when a goal finally arrived – and by that time there were 25 minutes left – the players who produced it were Souness and Dalglish … the former had had to bide his time for a place in the European matches and, as he told me, for him that season had been somehwat unreal, because he had been in and out of the side since his arrival from Middlesbrough. Now, though, he was to play a vital role and he received the ball, and delivered a perceptive pass into space. Dalglish, as Paisley had once told me, was already going for the ball even before it arrived, and from the right-hand side of the pitch he struck with deadly effect, to beat 'keeper Jensen. The only question remaining was whether or not Bruges could recover from the blow – they couldn't.

So Liverpool returned home with the trophy still in their possession, and as they celebrated themselves, Bob Paisley gave his opposite number at Nottingham Forest full credit for what he and his side had achieved. Brian Clough followed Paisley as Manager of the Year – after all, he had steered his team to a double – and when season 1978-79 kicked off, it was back to the grindstone for both clubs. There could be no looking back and living on past success … it was what you did from now on that counted. What Liverpool did, in the final analysis, was to regain their championship crown … what Forest did was to replace Liverpool as holders of the European Cup. And along the way, they knocked out Bob Paisley's team.

Three victories at the start of the season were followed by a League Cup knock-out, for Liverpool, as they lost against Sheffield United at Bramall Lane. Then, at the beginning of September, they demolished Tottenham Hotspur at Anfield as they scored seven goals without reply. It was one of Liverpool's most sparkling displays during the Paisley era – and there were more than a few. After Spurs, Liverpool travelled to Birmingham, where they registered a 3-0 victory … then they had to face up to Nottingham Forest, right at the start of their defence of the European Cup. Bob pulled his face a bit, when the European Cup pairings were made – as he told me, 'that's just what we didn't want to happen, right at the start … two English clubs coming up against each other'. But he had to accept the way the cookie had crumbled, and Liverpool's luck was most certainly out when they took on Forest in the first leg, which was at the City Ground … on September 13. Paisley's worst fears were justified as Forest forged a 2-0 lead on home territory; they managed a goal in each half, and so they went to Anfield brimming with confidence. In between the first and second legs, Liverpool had League games against Coventry City and West Brom, so it was Merseyside versus the Midlands all the way. Paisley saw his players beat Coventry and draw away against West Brom, and when the European Cup return came round, more than 51,000 people packed Anfield for this decider. Forest did what Liverpool had done so well and so often in these European confrontations – they kept their nerve and they defended with resolution; they did it so well that no matter how Liverpool tried – and try they did, as they threw on Fairclough and Johnson as substitutes – they found there was no way through. Forest didn't score, but they denied Liverpool even one goal.

Before the first leg, Paisley had refused to forecast the outcome … he said simply: 'We couldn't have been handed a tougher proposition than Forest … I don't think I can recall anything to measure up to a test such as this so early in the competition in the past. What I DO know is that if we knock Forest off the trail, we need have no fears about anyone else. They won't come any harder from anywhere on the Continent'. He was right about that, because by the end of the campaign Forest, by beating Malmo in the final, had proved themselves to be masters of anything Europe could put up against them. After the return match at Anfield – had Liverpool won, they would have been looking forward to their 100th match in their quest for one of the major European prizes – Paisley was his usual, inscrutable self, though disappointed to see his side knocked off the European trail. But, sportingly, he gave due credit to Forest. And, of course, he was prepared to battle on, in the search for success.

In the League, Liverpool beat Bolton Wanderers 3-0, Norwich City 4-1, Derby County 5-0 and Chelsea 2-0 in successive matches, leaving the fans to mutter that they wished just three of those 14 goals could have been put past Peter Shilton in the game against Forest. Everton halted Liverpool's run by winning the Goodison derby game 1-0, while Leeds United drew at Anfield; then there were victories over Queen's Park Rangers and Manchester City, a draw at Tottenham and a 2-0 home win over Middlesbrough before another defeat – 0-1 at Highbury. What was termed the European Super Competition brought a 3-1 defeat away against Anderlecht, then Liverpool scored a 2-0 victory over Forest in the League game at Anfield. There was a 1-0 reverse away against Bristol City, a 2-1 home win in the return against Anderlecht, and a comprehensive, 3-0 success against Manchester United at Old Trafford, to round off the first half of the season.

Liverpool were not to know then that United would be barring their way along the F.A. Cup trail to Wembley, come April; neither did they know that they would be driving for the championship, come the final weeks of the season. For the present, the accent switched to the F.A. Cup with the turn of the year, and after a scoreless draw at Southend, the replay ended with a comfortable, 3-0 result in Liverpool's favour.

January, 1979, was notable for the fact that Liverpool were able to get in only three matches, and all of these were in the F.A. Cup – after two tussles with Southend United, they tried conclusions with Blackburn Rovers at Anfield, and came through the fourth-round tie with a single-goal victory. Three League games at Anfield followed – against West Brom, Birmingham City and Norwich City – and these were all won. On the eve of the match against Norwich, Bob Paisley was spelling it out how he felt, after it had been suggested to him that his team had done the hard work and could look forward to a fairly easy programme for the remainder of the campaign. 'It's the so-called easy ones that always worry me!' Liverpool had beaten West Brom to go top of the First Division again, and he reminded people: 'When you're up against a top team, the motivation is easy – everyone is on his toes. It's when you think two points are there for the taking that application is required – and for 90 minutes'.

Ever the realist, Paisley pointed out that after the victory over West Brom there were still 40 points at stake – 'and, had I been asked then, I would have said I was looking for Liverpool to take 30 of those, which would make a total of 65.' He also made the point that 'I don't really expect any club this season to better that 67-point record haul by Leeds when they won the championship 10 years ago, and we finished second, with 61 points... In my opinion, it's going to take something like 65 points for a team to finish on top this season – and that's still some going, even allowing for the points the top clubs have picked up, so far'.

Liverpool's manager, still very much down to earth, stressed: 'But you cannot look for anything more than two points from your next match, and that's exactly what we shall be doing today'. At the end of the 90 minutes against Norwich, Paisley had seen his side score half a dozen goals without reply, to make sure of two more points. And he was not to know, then, that by the end of the League campaign Liverpool would have claimed the top spot – with 68 points, to set a new record. As for Nottingham Forest, after the key matches they had won against Liverpool, they would have to settle for second spot, eight points adrift.

CHAPTER 12

'I'm to blame'

BEFORE season 1978-79 had run its course, Bob Paisley was to be blaming himself for the fact that Liverpool missed out on the F.A. Cup, even if they scooped the League-title trophy. He was to suffer, as well as to savour success, because among the matches Liverpool played after their 6-0 hammering of Norwich City were two F.A. Cup semi-final duels with Manchester United, as well as the games which would decide the destination of the League championship. Immediately after the Norwich game came League matches against Derby County, Chelsea and Coventry City – all away – with a fifth-round F.A. Cup-tie against Burnley at Anfield sandwiched in between the trips to the Baseball Ground and Stamford Bridge. Derby were beaten, 2-0, and Burnley conceded three goals in the Cup-tie, while it was a 0-0 draw against Chelsea, and a similar scoreline when Liverpool met Coventry City at Highfield Road.

So Liverpool resumed their quest for F.A. Cup glory as they travelled to Portman Road, and a single-goal victory over Ipswich set them up not only for the semi-finals, but for a derby game against Everton in the League. At Anfield, Everton held their rivals to a 1-1 draw; but when Wolves and Ipswich played there in successive matches, they were each beaten, 2-0. Which left Liverpool looking at their next date … the F.A. Cup semi-final against Manchester United. It was scheduled for Maine Road on Saturday, March 31, and the scramble for tickets indicated the fierce interest the fans were taking in the match. From a Liverpool point of view, the Maine Road venue favoured United, since it was right on their doorstep.

Kenny Dalglish had been Liverpool's match-winner at Portman Road and against Blackburn Rovers; he had also been a marksman in the replay against Southend United … and he was first off the mark against Manchester United, at Maine Road, as he struck after the game had been going for no more than 17 minutes. However, this was to be no easy passage to Wembley, because United made Liverpool battle every inch of the way, and it was a goal by Alan Hansen, eight minutes from time, which made sure that the match must go to a replay. With the half-time score level at 1-1, the 52,000 fans inside the ground had plenty to talk about, and they had even more to debate as the venue was switched from Manchester to Merseyside … Everton's Goodison Park. Not surprisingly, the Liverpool contingent were confident that what amounted to home advantage would help their favourites to go marching on to Wembley. But it just didn't happen that way.

There were more than 53,000 people inside Goodison Park when the teams kicked off, and by half-time, with the game scoreless, it was obvious that one goal could be priceless. When it came, it was scored by Manchester United – and it was Bob Paisley who held a post-match inquest as he admitted that he had been guilty of a tactical error. Bob told me: 'I blamed myself because, having drawn 2-2 in the first game, I made a tactical switch for the replay which, later, I recognised had been a mistake. It wasn't individual players who were to blame – it was my own failure to stick with the style which suited us best. In game after game, we have shown that a 4-4-2 formation suited us best; that was the game we had perfected … yet on the night of the replay, and at Goodison Park, of all places, I switched to 4-3-3 – and we failed to translate pressure into goals. We paid the penalty – we let Manchester United break away and get one'.

Paisley declared afterwards that he should have been 'horse-whipped' for the decision he had made – 'I wasn't laying the blame on any player … I was blaming myself for the mistake which, deep down, I knew I had made even before the teams kicked off'. It was a pointed reminder for Bob that 'not for the first time since I became a manager, I had been made to recognise that it doesn't pay to depart from a formula which has proved to be the right one'. Yet there remained a silver lining to the cloud, because Paisley was able to declare that if the semi-final defeat had been a sickener, Liverpool still demonstrated their ability.

When it came to keeping going in the League, 'we proved that we were still the best team in the country … we scored a League double over United, beat Forest 2-0 in the League at Anfield and drew 0-0 against them on their own ground when a result for us – and them – was vital. Forest and West Brom were still in with a chance of the title, and we had three away matches on the trot, including the one against Forest. We got a 1-1 draw at Southampton, drew at Forest, then won 4-1 at Bolton'. As Paisley said, with four games still to go for Liverpool, time was running out for their rivals – and he declared defiantly, in any event, that 'we are prepared for a title fight to the finish!'

He pointed out that over the months since the turn of the year, it had been people outside Anfield who were talking about Liverpool winning the championship … 'I have always tried to point out that a race is never won until the finishing post has been passed, to use racing parlance. If it does turn out that Liverpool clinch the title with one or two games to go, that will be a bonus … but we are prepared for a fight to the finish. This season, while Liverpool have led the way for most of the time, I have always been well aware that forecasts don't guarantee fulfilment'. And he told the football world that 'while the title is the only thing left to us now, it is not our priority – our aim is simply to win points from each game as it comes along. And when we've played them all, we'll know whether or not we've done enough'.

After that 4-1 win at Burnden Park against Bolton, Liverpool had four games left: against Southampton, Aston Villa, Middlesbrough and Leeds United. They were indeed on the verge of being crowned League champions … four matches to go, and a seven-point lead, although Nottingham Forest and West Brom each had a game in hand. However, they needed to win every time out, to stand a chance of catching Paisley's team. And when Liverpool defeated Southampton 2-0 at Anfield, they knew that all they required was a draw from their home game against Aston Villa on May 8 … which just happened to be the 40th anniversry of Paisley's arrival as a young hopeful at Anfield.

It was a date for Bob Paisley to remember, and not solely because Liverpool had an important match … their manager also had a date with the dentist, that afternoon. So he had to sandwich this visit in between his preparations for the game and his team talk that Tuesday evening. As events turned out, it became the night that Liverpool won the League championship for the 11th time in their history, to set a record in English football. Liverpool did it in some style, too, because they scored three goals without reply, and at the end it was Paisley's turn to go out on to the pitch and raise his arms as he acknowledged the cheers of the massed ranks of the Anfield faithful.

The supporters had been waiting for the Anfield gates to open two and a half hours before kick-off time, and when the teams lined up, it was in front of more than 50,000 people. As Paisley admitted later: 'The mood was one of eager anticipation, the champagne was on ice … but I had one gnawing doubt. Would Villa (who had won at Anfield the previous season and who had beaten Liverpool 3-1 in the mid-April duel) spoil the party? – Everyone knew the title was there for the taking, but deep down, I had the secret fear that it might still all prove to be a big let-down on the night'. And even when Alan Kennedy scored the first goal, after only 47 seconds had gone by, Liverpool's manager was still wondering if it was going to be 'too good to be true'.

His fcars proved to be groundless, because Liverpool took a grip on the game, and when Dalglish – voted the Football Writers' Player of the Year – made it 2-0 just before half-time, the writing was on the wall for Villa. Terry McDermott's second-half goal killed the game stone dead as a contest, and the Kop was in full cry as the fans raised their voices to roar: 'Nottingham Forest, you're not champions any more!' Then they chanted 'Hand it over! Hand it over!' – meaning, of course, the championship trophy, and towards the end of the 90 minutes they sang You'll Never walk Alone, and began to call out the name of Bob Paisley. When Dalglish missed a scoring chance, the Kop's sense of humour broke through, once again… 'What a waste of money! … 'was the cry. Liverpool had claimed back the title trophy, and done it with something to spare, because they still had games to play against Middlesbrough and Leeds, although both these fixtures were away from home.

Victory at Ayresome Park meant that Liverpool needed to win their final match, at Elland Road, if they were to total 68 points and thus overhaul the record set by Leeds themselves a decade earlier; and they did the trick by scoring three goals. Two of them came from David Johnson, and Jimmy Case chipped in with one which earned the club a £50,000 prize – because that second goal meant Liverpool had hit an 84-goal target. Liverpool's 3-0 victory, indeed, set two new records, because as well as achieving the highest-ever points tally, they finished up with the record of having conceded the fewest goals, as the final League placing showed. It read: Played 42, Won 30, Drawn 8, Lost 4, Goals for 85, Goals against 16, Points 68. The final accolade came when Paisley himself was named Manager of the Year – for the third time in four seasons … and that, of course, was yet another record.

The man who, at the age of 55, had become a reluctant hero was coming towards the close of an outstanding managerial career; and yet, during the next few seasons, he demonstrated once again that he still possessed that capacity to produce winning teams. If season 1978-79 had seemed to cap what had gone before, at least in some respects, there were to be more seasons of success – almost a hat-trick of League championships (three League titles in four seasons), a hat-trick of League-Milk Cup triumphs, and a third European Cup success. Indeed, the remarkable Paisley was to round of his glittering career with a double.

CHAPTER 13

European Hat-Trick

TWO CLUBS – one from London and one from the far-flung province of Georgia, in what was then the Soviet Union – put paid to Bob Paisley's hopes of achieving another European Cup triumph and a first-ever F.A. Cup success under his management for Liverpool, in season 1979-80. Not that he could grumble, because when all the League points had been totted up, once again it was the Anfield club which led the way. In Europe, however, after the bitter disappointment of an early exit against Nottingham Forest the previous season, it came as a double blow when Dynamo Tbilisi became one of the handful of clubs to defeat Liverpool at such a stage in European competition. And in the F.A. Cup, it was Arsenal who survived what became a marathon, semi-final battle for the right to march on to Wembley. If there was some consolation, it lay in the fact that along the way, Liverpool managed to get the better of Nottingham Forest in the F.A. Cup … although in the semi-finals of the League Cup it was Forest who triumphed against them yet again.

The season began on a quiet note, as Liverpool could do no better than draw against Bolton Wanderers at Anfield and, after a 3-1 home win against West Brom, they had to settle for a scoreless draw against Tranmere Rovers in the League Cup match at Prenton Park. There followed a 3-2 defeat at Southampton, then Tranmere and Coventry City in turn felt the weight of Liverpool's punching power as each team succumbed to a four-goal mauling. The European Cup was next on the Anfield agenda, and Liverpool squeezed home by a 2-1 margin, thanks to first-half goals from David Johnson and Jimmy Case, but any hopes that this would be a sufficient lead were swiftly snuffed out.

After a home draw against Norwich and a 3-1 League Cup win over Chesterfield, Liverpool went into the the return European game on the back of a 1-0 defeat in the League at Nottingham Forest's City Ground, and the long and tiring trip to Georgia saw Tbilisi really putting the skids under Paisley's side as Dynamo scored three times, while Liverpool failed to register one shot on target. There was a crowd of 80,000 to witness this demolition job on a team which had carried off the European Cup twice, and it was not a happy experience for Paisley's men to be beaten at the outset for the second season in succession. Still, the League did provide some cause for cheer, as Bristol City suffered, being hammered 4-0, and Manchester City had to ensure a similar fate – including the scoreline – at Maine Road. In the fourth round of the League Cup, Exeter City went down 2-0, then Liverpool maintained their scoring touch as they beat Wolves 3-0, Brighton 4-1 and Spurs 2-1.

There was a foretaste of what was to come in the F.A. Cup as Liverpool travelled to London and drew 0-0 against Arsenal at Highbury, then they rattled in four goals against Middlesbrough at Anfield, won the fifth-round tie against Norwich City in the League Cup with a convincing, 3-1 scoreline at Carrow Road, and disposed of Aston Villa in the League in similar fashion. Crystal Palace went down 3-0, Derby County lost 3-1, and Liverpool made it six wins on the trot as Manchester United were beaten 2-0 at Anfield. They did the same to West Brom away, and that took them to the end of the year. In 17 matches since their European Cup exit, Liverpool had scored no fewer than 44 goals and had failed to hit the target only once – at Highbury. In those 17 games they had conceded just nine goals, and kept nine clean sheets. That was an impressive record with which to embark upon the New Year.

Grimsby Town were the first victims – they went down 5-0 in the third round of the F.A. Cup, at Anfield, but then came a change of fortune for Liverpool as Southampton drew 1-1 at Anfield and Coventry City won 1-0 at Highfield Road. Liverpool had to travel to Nottingham for the first leg of their League Cup semi-final against Forest, and they returned knowing they must wipe out a 1-0 deficit, if they were to reach Wembley; in the event, a Fairclough goal one minute from time in the Anfield return snatched a draw there – so Forest marched on … and they were paired with Liverpool in the fourth round of the F.A. Cup, as well.

One way and another, the team that Brian Clough had moulded was proving to be a real thorn in Liverpool's side, and the trip back to the City Ground had many of the Liverpool supporters fearing the worst once more. It didn't happen this time, though – goals from Dalglish after half an hour and McDermott (a penalty with 20 minutes to go) ended Forest's interest in the F.A. Cup, and Liverpool honour had been satisfied. They also earned plaudits for a handsome, 5-3 victory at Norwich in the League, and when Forest played at Anfield for the points, they were beaten 2-0, immediately after the fifth round of the F.A. Cup, in which Liverpool saw off Bury, with a 2-0 win at Anfield. Just before the sixth round – Liverpool were paired with Tottenham Hotspur – Paisley's men went to Goodison Park and scored a 2-1 success, to set them up for the Cup duel, and at White Hart Lane, in front of a crowd of more than 48,000, Liverpool pursued their quest for the classic League-F.A. Cup double as McDermott's first-half goal proved to be the difference between the teams.

Manchester City, Bristol City, Leeds United and Brighton all fell to Liverpool in League games, but Spurs managed to win that battle at White Hart Lane, and after victories over Stoke City and Derby County (sandwiched by a defeat at the hands of Manchester United at Old Trafford), the next stop was Hillsborough – not for a date with Sheffield Wednesday, but for the semi-final of the F.A. Cup against Arsenal. It was a match which drew a gate of more than 50,000, and the spectators saw a ding-dong battle … but no goals. So they made the trek to Villa Park for the replay, where by half-time they were still waiting to see the ball enter the net. Liverpool's David Fairclough obliged soon after the restart, by 90 minutes the score was 1-1, and that was how it stayed, once extra time had been completed. The first match had been played on April 12, the replay had taken place on April 16, and now a second replay was scheduled at Villa Park for April 28. By half-time, Arsenal fans were smiling; their team was a goal ahead … and with one minute left, it looked as if Liverpool were down and about to go out. But that old fighting spirit came to their rescue, and it was Dalglish who, almost on the final whistle, snatched the goal which once again took the semi-final into extra time. And once again, another 30 minutes failed to produce an outright winner. As if this were not enough, Arsenal had paid a visit to Anfield straight after the first replay, and held Liverpool to a 1-1 draw in the League. By the time the second replay had ended, the teams were almost sick of the sight of each other.

Liverpool were still going for the League championship, as well, and they were running out of games … after the home draw with Arsenal they won 2-0 at Stoke and drew 0-0 away with Crystal Palace, before plunging into that second F.A. Cup replay … and, as had happened just one year earlier, Aston Villa were the visitors to Anfield early in May, for the final home League match of the campaign. But two days before that May 3 date, Liverpool and Arsenal had to meet each other in a third replay, this time at Highfield Road … and, at long, long last, there was a result. Sadly, after all their prodigious efforts, it was not to be Liverpool manager Bob Paisley who led out his team to Wembley … the Gunners scored the only goal, in the first half, and they managed to cling to their slender advantage to the end. That marathon, F.A. Cup duel had been seen by more than 169,000 people, altogether, as it see-sawed through 420 minutes of action. And it was a testimony to Liverpool's staying power that as they fought and fought, they also managed to stay on course for the title. After their exertions against the Gunners, they braced themselves for the last two games – Villa at Anfield, Middlesbrough at Ayresome Park … and a comprehensive, 4-1 win over Villa, in front of more than 51,000 fans, finally brought reward, in the shape of the title trophy. The fact that Liverpool lost at Middlesbrough three days later was of no real significance.

If Liverpool had missed out on a double, one of their players – Terry McDermott – had achieved one … he was voted the Sportswriters' Footballer of the Year and the PFA Player of the Year. Liverpool had staved off the championship challenge of Manchester United, and their players had clocked up new landmarks in their careers... Ray Clemence had played in his 50th F.A. Cup-tie and totalled 600 games for Liverpool; Phil Thompson (about to complete 350 appearances), Phil Neal and Kenny Dalglish had been ever-presents, while Dalglish was heading also for his 500th game, with Celtic and Liverpool. Ray Kennedy had taken his Liverpool tally to 300 appearances, David Johnson had topped the century mark for League games, and Graeme Souness was heading for 100 appearances. It all added up to a remarkable record of consistency, both individually and collectively. And there was more to come ... although, having clinched the championship, Liverpool were about to see Aston Villa take the title trophy 12 months later and succeed them two years hence as the champions of Europe.

The Paisley pattern of success was repeated, though, in season 1980-81; because Liverpool went through more than 60 matches to emerge with the European Cup for the third time in the club's history. In the F.A. Cup, their progress was halted by Everton in round four – a 2-1 defeat at Goodison Park followed the 4-1 home victory over non-Leaguers Altrincham in the third round. It became a season of the double, however, as Liverpool claimed the League Cup, with a replay victory over West Ham at Villa Park. In the League, they ended up by lagging behind the likes of champions Aston Villa, Ipswich Town and Arsenal – but nobody at Anfield was shedding tears, considering that two trophies were on the sideboard. Yet the League Cup campaign had begun with a shock result – a 1-0 defeat at Bradford City's ground, although the team from Yorkshire paid for their temerity when they played at Anfield in the second leg. Dalglish (two goals), Ray Kennedy and Johnson made it a Liverpool victory, 4-1 on aggregate.

Swindon Town went to Anfield and fared even worse than Bradford City, since Liverpool stuck five goals past them – well, four goals (Sammy Lee two goals, Dalglish and Fairclough), because Glenn Cockerill put through his own goal. Then Liverpool's luck was in again, as they were paired with Portsmouth on home ground – and the fans of Pompey travelled to Anfield in numbers for this match. They saw Liverpool in merciless mood ... while Portsmouth scored once, their opponents struck four times (Johnson twice, Dalglish, Souness), and so it was on to the next round, with a tie against Birmingham City. At half-time, with the score 1-1, the issue remained uncertain; but by 90 minutes McDermott and Johnson had added to the early goal from Dalglish, and all was well that ended well ... but as Liverpool moved smoothly into the semi-finals, they knew that they were up against tough opposition – their rivals from Maine Road, Manchester City.

If Liverpool had looked upon Maine Road as a happy hunting ground for them, by the same token City had turned in some sterling displays at Anfield, and Bob Paisley knew well enough that nothing could be taken for granted. The first leg was away, which suited Liverpool, with their vast experience of two-legged ties in Europe, and they contained the City attacks, then struck for goal themselves. Nine minutes from the final whistle, Ray Kennedy did the damage, and left the 48,000 onlookers pondering upon City's chance of springing an upset in the return.

More than 46,000 people flocked to Anfield to see what would happen and the Liverpool faithful were rewarded by seeing Dalglish score inside 25 minutes, to give their team a 2-0 aggregate advantage; but when City broke through and made it 1-1 on the night, hearts were in mouths as the minutes ticked away towards the final whistle. It didn't come a moment too soon for the home supporters, but at last they could relax ... Liverpool were on their way to Wembley again, there to meet West Ham, who were rated the under-dogs. The 100,000 crowd watched and waited, but by half-time a goal hadn't been scored, and the same applied after 90 minutes; so the final went into extra time, and with 118 minutes on the clock overall, it was Barney Rubble – alias Alan Kennedy – who struck for Liverpool. To Liverpool's consternation, however, West Ham also got their names on the scoresheet ... as Ray Stewart scored from the penalty spot.

There was no doubt about one thing – Liverpool's players and their manager left Wembley with the feeling that they should have been taking the League Cup with them, despite the effort the Hammers had put in. Liverpool fans were sure, too, that their team had done more than enough to claim victory. But it was goals that counted, and now it remained to be seen if Liverpool could muster enough to win the replay at Villa Park ... a replay which had to wait until the first day of April, after the final which had been played on March 14. Would it be a case of April Fool? – No-one knew the answer, of course, as Liverpool tackled three other teams between the Wembley final and the Villa Park replay. In the European Cup it was CSKA Sofia; in the League it was Everton at Anfield and Arsenal at Highbury; and each time the scoreline finished 1-0, with Liverpool losing out to the Gunners, but winning the other two games.

In Sofia, Liverpool had played in front of a crowd of 60,000; at Anfield, for the derby game, there was a gate of close on 50,000; and at Highbury, more than 47,000 people turned up to see the action. The Villa Park attendance dipped ... after 100,000 at Wembley, there were just under 37,000 spectators for the replay; not surprising, considering the money Liverpool fans had had to fork out for the trip into Europe and the other matches they had watched during a hectic season. The final replay would be the 51st match of the season for Liverpool – and there were still 11 more games to go.

Liverpool rang the changes, for the replay. Ray Clemence, Phil Neal and

Alan Kennedy were still there, but in the back-four line Phil Thompson replaced Colin Irwin; and while other familiar names remained… Ray Kennedy, Alan Hansen, Kenny Dalglish, Sammy Lee and Terry McDermott, the names of Steve Heighway and Graeme Souness were replaced on the teamsheet by those of a newcomer, Ian Rush, and Jimmy Case. Irwin landed a place on the bench. Of course, you could always anticipate a goal from Dalglish, but you seldom expected the elegant Hansen to be a marksman for Liverpool – his place was at the heart of the defence, and only rarely did he make a foray forward. However, at Villa Park, while Dalglish did the business once again, after the game had been going for 25 minutes, Hansen turned out to be Liverpool's match-winner … three minutes after the goal from Dalglish, his fellow-Scot was on the mark. Since West Ham were restricted to one goal, the brace from Liverpool was enough, and so the League Cup took its place on the Anfield sideboard – or, to be precise, in the trophy room.

By that time, Liverpool were aiming to complete a Cup double, with the European trophy as their second target, and they had advanced to the semi-final stage of that competition by virtue of victories over Oulu Palloseura, from Finland; the champions of Scotland, Aberdeen; and the Bulgarian champions, CSKA Sofia. Bayern Munich, from West Germany, provided stiff opposition for the Reds from Anfield in the penultimate round of the tournament. Oulu had held Liverpool to a draw – 1-1 – on their own patch in Finland, but when the part-timers tried their luck at Anfield they were given a real hiding. The goals went in, one after the other … hat-tricks from both Graeme Souness (5, 24, 52 minutes – the third one a penalty) and Terry McDermott (29, 41, 83), two goals from David Fairclough (68, 81), and the remainder from Sammy Lee and Ray Kennedy. Oulu's goalkeeper was seldom out of action, though the Finns did manage one in reply.

A McDermott strike sank Aberdeen in the first leg at Pittodrie, and Liverpool scored four goals without reply in the Anfield return (kicking off with an own goal from Willie Miller, then tacking on goals from Neal, Dalglish and Hansen). When CSKA Sofia visited Anfield, the tie was as good as settled inside an hour, and Souness walked off the park being hailed as a hat-trick hero.

He opened the scoring after 16 minutes, added goals after 51 and 80 minutes; meanwhile, Lee had made it 2-0 five minutes before half-time and McDermott had scored with the hour just gone by. So the aggregate score finished up at 6-1, since CSKA scored once, though they couldn't even do this as Johnson ensured a single-goal victory for Liverpool in the away leg. After CSKA, however, Bayern Munich looked like providing much sterner opposition, and in front of 44,000 fans at Anfield, they showed they hadn't come to roll over and die. They went away with a 0-0 scoreline to their credit, and at least one of their players claimed that they had done the hard part. At half-time in the return match, there still wasn't a goal between the teams, but when Bayern did forge ahead, it seemed as if they were on their way to the final in Paris. The crowd of 77,600 – most of them, at any rate – thought so … but Liverpool played an ace twice over, as Bob Paisley sent on winger Howard Gayle for Dalglish – then substituted Gayle by sending on Case. Gayle, however, had given Bayern plenty to think about during his spell in action, and with seven minutes to go it was Ray Kennedy who pulled the chestnuts out of the fire as he made the aggregate score 1-1. That away goal counted double for Liverpool … they were through to the final.

It was staged in the Parc des Princes, in Paris, on May 27, in front of 48,000 spectators – none more committed than the Liverpool contingent. The opposition came from those giants of the tournament, Real Madrid, and they had the German, Uli Stielike, in their ranks, along with an Englishman – winger Laurie Cunningham, who had made his name with West Brom. It was a final in which Paisley and his team wrote their name into the record books – they might not have lifted the trophy as often as their illustrious opponents, but they earned their third success in the competition, which was more than any other British club had managed. Indeed, Nottingham Forest had carried on where Liverpool left off, the previous term, and Aston Villa were to follow Liverpool as European champions. But before that, there was this final of 1981, and for quite a while it seemed as if it was going to be something of a let-down all round. Real defended in depth, Liverpool's 'keeper was seldom tested, although early on he did have to deal with a cross from Cunningham. Real 'keeper Agustin saved from Dalglish and Alan Kennedy, while Ray Kennedy and McDermott drove the ball wide.

The second half followed the pattern of the first, to a large degree, with Real attempting to stifle their opponents by man-to-man marking; and when McDermott finally managed to weave his way through, he went down on the edge of the penalty box under a challenge from an opponent by the name of… Angel. When Real at last managed to make a break for it, Comacho lobbed an effort goalwards, only to see it sail just over the bar, and by the time the game had entered the last 10 minutes, neutral observers were just wishing that someone – anyone – would score a goal. It finally arrived, and Ray Kennedy began the move. As Sammy Lee shaped to take a throw, Kennedy took over, for he reckoned that he could land the ball deeper into Real's territory. He was right, because the throw-in reached Alan Kennedy, and the man the fans loved to see racing down the left flank belted a fierce left-foot shot past the startled Agustin. The Liverpool supporters roared 'Barney Rubble! Barney Rubble!' as they hailed their hero, and so the European Cup had been won and lost. Bob Paisley and his team had completed yet another sensational double and, once again, people were asking how even Liverpool and their manager could follow that.

Steve Nicol in action against Tony Cottee in a Liverpool derby game.
Another of Paisley's signings, Nicol was one of the most versatile
defenders ever to play at Liverpool.

CHAPTER 14

A Nail-Biting Affair

IT WAS mid-January, 1982, and Liverpool were due to meet Wolves at Anfield. The weather was playing havoc with the fixture list, and only five First Division games got the go-ahead. Liverpool's was one … yet, at that stage of the season, as Bob Paisley said, 'many people have written Liverpool out of their calculations so far as the championship is concerned'. He added: 'And I am not going to start shouting the odds about our chances, just to be different'. What he did admit was that he was concerned about club's League position – they stood ninth in the table – 'because our progress in the bread-and-butter matches, week by week, is the one real yardstick to measure our consistency. Obviously, I would be happy if Liverpool won a trophy in one of the Cup competitions … equally obviously, I am aware that we have left ourselves an awful lot to do, when it comes to winning the First Division title'. Yet, he said, 'my priority is the League – and if it's still possible for us to win it, then that's what our aim must be'.

At the top of the table stood Ipswich Town and Manchester City, each eight points clear of Paisley's team – and while City had played 21 matches, Ipswich had played only 17, one match fewer than Liverpool. By the end of that Saturday in January, Ipswich were three points better off, after a victory at Coventry, and Liverpool had climbed to seventh spot, after having beaten Wolves. But above them, Ipswich apart, there remained what Paisley termed 'formidable opposition' … the two Manchester clubs and Nottingham Forest, for instance. However, by the time Liverpool were meeting Tottenham Hotspur at Anfield in mid-May, the League table had a different look about it – and Liverpool had already lifted the League Cup … after victory over Spurs at Wembley.

On the day that Liverpool tangled again with Tottenham, in that penultimate League match of the season, Paisley's team stood proudly at the top of the table – 83 points in the bag, two games to go; while Ipswich had two matches left, and they lagged by three points. Manchester United, in third place, had two games left, but no hope – they had mustered only 72 points, while fourth-placed Spurs were playing for their pride at Anfield, even though they had four games left. But they had totalled just 70 points. Bob Paisley was able to claim that as the last lap came into view, 'the race for the championship has narrowed to such an extent that it lies between ourselves and Ipswich, and it reinforces the view I held and expressed at a time when people were writing us out of the title fight.

I used to tell the players that I still hadn't seen a team to better Liverpool, on our day; and I rammed it home, time and time again, that the title was still there to be won. Well, we're going for three points against Spurs and three against Middlesbrough at Ayresome next Tuesday night; and for the simple reason that this is the Liverpool way. It's an attitude of mind which has carried us through a few crises and on to a good many successes. Now, we hope, it will bring us the title'. And, of course, Bob Paisley was right.

The 48,000 fans who packed Anfield saw Liverpool turn on a three-goal display as they shot down Spurs… Lawrenson, Whelan and Dalglish were the marksmen, and the title trophy was coming back to Anfield from its temporary home at Villa Park. A scoreless draw at Middlesbrough wrapped up the campaign and left Paisley once more a happy man. Once more, also, Liverpool had demonstrated that they had the staying power to come through more than 60 matches, at home and in Europe, and finish up with something to show for their efforts … even if they had kicked off by losing 1-0 against Wolves at Molineux, and only drawing, 1-1, with Middlesbrough at Anfield. Once again, in Europe, they had tackled the Finns of Oulu Palloseura and beaten them 7-0 at Anfield, while in the League Cup they had rammed five goals past the luckless Exeter City. They had shared half a dozen goals in the exhilarating League game at Brighton's Goldstone Ground, and come away from Holland with a 2-2 draw against AZ'67 Alkmaar in the second round of the European Cup. They followed up a 2-1 home defeat at the hands of Manchester United by going to Exeter for the League Cup return and knocking in half a dozen goals, and they won in the League at Sunderland.

Some games linger long in the memory, and when Liverpool met AZ'67 Alkmaar in the Anfield return, on the night of Wednesday, November 4, 1981, that match was one of them … and not just because it turned out to be a tense, nerve-wracking and nail-biting affair for Paisley and his side. It was a match I shall always remember – and with special reason; because it was a night I could so easily have died. As usual, I had driven the 20-odd miles to Liverpool from my home, parked the car a few hundred yards from the ground and, in company with hundreds of other people, I set off to complete the journey to Liverpool's ground. It was a bitterly-cold night, and you needed to walk at a pretty fast pace to counter the conditions and, as I walked, I passed some people, while others were going even faster than me.

Suddenly, I felt a searing pain start in the centre of my chest, and it spread within mere seconds. I wondered what had hit me, the pain was so agonising … in fact, after only a few paces, I simply had to stop. I didn't know what the fans going past me thought, as I came to a sudden halt, but I know what I felt like – I could hardly breathe. As I stood there, I wondered if I should retrace my steps to the car and return home; then I reflected that if I did this, there would be questions from my wife as to why I was back so soon … and I didn't want to worry her unduly. I waited for a minute or two, then I tried a tentative step. I could still feel the effects of the pain, but I managed to get going once more, though I was walking so slowly, gingerly putting one foot in front of the other, and I must have looked like an old man of 100, had anyone stopped to look at me. I figured that if I could reach the sanctuary of the Anfield Press box – my usual spot for watching the matches – I would be able to sit quietly and spend the rest of the evening recovering from whatever it was that had struck.

Slowly, ever so slowly, I made my way forward and, eventually, I got to the ground. It had taken me so long that by the time I arrived it was almost time for the teams to be out on the field for the pre-match kickabout. Hesitantly, I made my way up the steps from the main entrance, took my place in the Press box, and got my breath back – although when I thought of that terrible pain, my chest seemed so tight. Whether it was the fact that Liverpool were considered to be virtually home and dry, I don't know; but the gate was nothing exceptional.

When the teams kicked off, there were fewer than 30,000 people inside Anfield … and they were in for a shock. Liverpool might have scored two goals in the away leg, to come out of that match with a 2-2 result, and by half-time in the return game it was the home supporters who were feeling optimistic, because their favourites had taken a 1-0 lead to go ahead 3-2 on aggregate and, of course, their away goals meant that Liverpool were now well and truly in the driving seat. Or so it seemed, after Terry McDermott had struck from the penalty spot with the interval only three minutes away. I stayed in the Press box throughout the interval, rather than venturing into the hospitality room for a cup of tea, and all around the Liverpool fans were eagerly anticipating the second half and the ultimate success of Bob Paisley's team.

The second half turned out to be one in which many of the Anfield faithful must have become candidates for heart attacks, as the game see-sawed and the result hung in the balance, because Alkmaar managed to find the Liverpool net not once, but twice – and there were visions of a genuine upset as the game progressed. Nerves were settled somewhat, because Ian Rush got his name on the scoresheet, but with only five minutes to go it was left to a defender – Alan Hansen – to deliver the decisive blow and give his side the edge by the odd goal in nine, overall. That second half was certainly no spectacle for faint-hearts, and I was feeling the strain probably more than anyone, after what had happened to me on the way to the ground.

By the time that Liverpool played their next European Cup match – against CSKA Sofia at the beginning of March, I had been in hospital and emerged safely, after open-heart surgery, and I had been informed that the blocked artery which had caused all the trouble could so easily had finished me off as I was walking to Liverpool's ground that November night. My luck had indeed been in, because it seemed that more often than not, people suffering as I had been suffering simply dropped dead on the spot ... fortunately for me, I was able to undergo surgery in quick time, and so I lived to tell the tale. In fact, I was in the operating theatre round about kick-off time on Saturday, November 28, 1981, and I wasn't fully aware of what was going on until some 24 hours later.

I learned that while I had been undergoing surgery the previous afternoon, Liverpool had been given some shock treatment at the hands of Southampton, who had been led out at Anfield by their skipper ... a fellow by the name of Kevin Keegan. The Saints had walked off the pitch as winners after 90 minutes, courtesy of a goal from Steve Moran. Like I said, some football matches tend to linger in the memory ... and you could class Liverpool's next outings in the Champions Cup among them. The previous season, when CSKA Sofia had tried conclusions with Paisley's side, they had walked off the pitch on the wrong end of a 5-1 scoreline, with Graeme Souness taking the individual honours after having scored a hat-trick. So it wasn't surprising that the home supporters envisaged another free-scoring romp for their favourites. One man who didn't believe this – and he said so, too – was Liverpool's manager.

Paisley issued a warning before the game when he declared that the previous time the teams had met, 'just about everything went right for us ... the scoreline made our opponents appear to be a worse side than they really were'. In fact, Paisley reckoned that far from this being an easy match, 'for my money, it's going to be HARDER'. He reminded the home fans that while Liverpool by then had reached the final of the League Cup, 'we haven't won anything yet – so that's all the more reason for us to pull out the stops tonight'. And he gave the Anfield fans another pointed reminder ... 'our experience in the F.A. Cup a few weeks ago should serve to make us wary'. Liverpool had gone to Swansea in the third round of that competition, and won comfortably, 4-0; then they had taken on Sunderland at Roker Park and scored three more goals, again without reply; but they had been well and truly sunk when they met Chelsea in the fifth round at Stamford Bridge, as they lost 2-0 to lose interest, also, in the F.A. Cup for another season.

The Bulgarians came to Anfield as League champions in successive seasons, and they had more or less the same squad of players that they had had a year earlier – which meant, as Paisley pointed out, that they were that much more experienced. They had competed in Europe through two decades, beaten Nottingham Forest the previous term, and so they had shown they could get results, even if they hadn't pulled up any trees by disposing of Real Sociedad and Glentoran before coming up against Liverpool for the second time around.

In the event, Paisley's warning turned out to have been well justified, because this time out there was no nap hand of goals for the home side – instead, the first half remained scoreless, and the fans had to wait until the 66th minute before they could raise their voices as Ronnie Whelan put Liverpool ahead. That was it, however, Liverpool walked off the pitch at the end knowing they had the slimmest of leads for the return match, which was scheduled to be played a fortnight later; and when Paisley's team played in Sofia, they found that the going was more than hard … not a goal after 45 minutes; not a goal – for them – after 90 minutes. But CSKA had struck one, which meant that now the match must go into extra time – the last thing Liverpool wanted, after their exertions in the League Cup final at Wembley four days earlier, and the prospect of a long flight back and then a difficult game against Sunderland on the Saturday. Extra time did prove decisive, and it didn't come down to away goals counting double or to penalty shoot-outs… CSKA scored the killer goal during the extra period, and so Liverpool made their exit, beaten 2-1 on aggregate.

They had the consolation of knowing that four days previously, they had picked up a trophy which would ensure they returned to European competition the following season, and they were still striving to take the League title; but defeat by CSKA Sofia had been a blow to their hopes of another Champions Cup triumph. As for the League Cup, they had made steady progress by way of trips to Barnsley and Ipswich, after the 11-0 demolition job on Exeter City at the start of the trail which had led to Wembley. The 4-1 victory over Middlesbrough at Anfield in round three was followed by a 0-0 draw at Highbury and a 3-0 victory over Arsenal in the Anfield replay, then came the trip to Barnsley's Oakwell ground after a scoreless draw at Anfield. This, of course, had been seen as a tricky test, but Liverpool conquered their opponents 3-1 and so they were through to the semi-finals, with a trip to Portman Road for the first leg against Ipswich. This was the first of three matches against Ipswich in succession – the Anfield League game was sandwiched between the two League Cup duels – and at Portman Road goals from Rush and McDermott virtually put Ipswich out of the hunt. That 2-0 win was followed by a 4-0 hiding for Ipswich in the League at Anfield, although they managed to hold Liverpool to a 2-2 draw in the League Cup second leg.

By that time, it was early February, and immediately after having reached the final of the League Cup, Liverpool were despatched from the F.A. Cup at Stamford Bridge – and then they lost 2-0 in the League at Swansea. They recovered to beat Coventry City 4-0 at Anfield, travelled to Elland Road and won 2-0 against Leeds United, followed their 1-0 home win over CSKA Sofia by losing 1-0 against Brighton, and hammered Stoke City 5-1 as a pipe-opener to their Wembley date with Tottenham Hotspur in the League Cup. And that match turned out to be a personal landmark in the career of Ronnie Whelan. Spurs had a record of success at Wembley – they had never yet lost a Cup final there; and they looked odds-on winners again when the game had no more than three minutes to go. In goal, former Liverpool star Ray Clemence had stopped everything they could throw at him, and the goal scored by Steve Archibald, after only 11 minutes, was still looking the one which would take the League Cup back to White Hart Lane.

As Spurs supporters willed the referee to blow for time, Liverpool mounted one more attack, and it was David Johnson – who had replaced Terry McDermott – who supplied the pass which Whelan drove home to take the game into extra time. Sammy Lee had gone close to scoring, shortly after the Tottenham goal, while Clemence had stopped McDermott and Dalglish from getting their names on the scoresheet as Liverpool drove forward in the second half. Yet even while Liverpool gained control during the extra period, with Tottenham visibly wilting under the pressure, the final had no more than nine minutes left before the referee would blow and the teams would be facing each other again in a replay at Villa Park.

Liverpool, however, still had the bit between their teeth, and they continued to put pressure on the Tottenham defence, which was tired and was becoming somewhat desperate to keep the ball away from goal. When Dalglish delivered a cross, one of the Spurs defenders tried to get to the ball and make yet another clearance, but he succeeded only in diverting the ball to Whelan. The Irishman was almost able to pick his spot, as he shot for goal, and Clemence was beaten for a second time. Now Tottenham had to forget all about keeping Liverpool out; they had to push forward themselves and risk leaving gaps at the back as they went for an equaliser.

It was the sort of situation which a side like Liverpool, experienced in all the arts of defending and counter-attacking, could turn to their advantage. And that was exactly what happened, because Liverpool broke once more and, with the Tottenham defence leaving gaps, Ian Rush delivered the killer blow, as he found himself in space, and with time to beat his one-time team-mate. Once again, Liverpool had demonstrated that a match is never won until the final whistle has gone, that a seemingly lost cause can be retrieved not just at the 11th hour, but in the dying minutes. Bob Paisley had now spent seven years as Liverpool's manager, and this League Cup triumph was the club's seventh major trophy success during that time. And even then, Liverpool were going to cap it all by claiming back the championship trophy, as the season came to its close.

There wasn't much time to dwell on the Wembley success, however, as the trip to Sofia for the European return loomed, and after that let-down the League matches followed almost non-stop, or so it seemed. There were three games left in March, six to be played in April, and another half-dozen to be got through between the first day of May and the extended end to the League season, May 18. Liverpool may have had to abandon hopes of a return to Wembley for the F.A. Cup final on May 22, but they had plenty on their plate if they were to add the championship trophy to the League Cup. Sunderland at Anfield came after the Bulgarian trip, and a goal from Rush ensured the points; then there was the testing visit across Stanley Park for the derby game against Everton, and Liverpool could thank marksmen Whelan, Johnston and Souness for delivering a 3-1 victory. It was 3-1 against Birmingham City and 1-0 against Notts County (both at Anfield), 1-0 against Manchester United at Old Trafford, then Liverpool had a 5-0 field-day against Manchester City at Maine Road, where Neal, Alan Kennedy, Rush, Lee and Johnston rattle in the nap hand of goals.

Kennedy and Johnston scored in the next match, too; a 2-0 victory over Stoke City at Anfield, while Dalglish was the single-goal match-winner against West Brom; and a brace of goals from Whelan, plus one from Rush, saw off Southampton 3-2 at The Dell. Liverpool now were down to their last half-dozen matches, against Nottingham Forest, Spurs, Birmingham, Arsenal, Spurs again and Middlesbrough. They were about to complete a 15-match run without a single defeat.

In those 15 games, Liverpool totalled 29 goals, conceded eight, and kept no fewer than nine clean sheets. Nottingham Forest, so often a thorn in Liverpool's side, were beaten 2-0 at Anfield, and Tottenham Hotspur, vanquished at Wembley, were held to a 2-2 draw on their own ground. That was the first of three away games on the trot, and at Birmingham a goal from Rush stole the points, while at Highbury it was Rushy on the mark once more, to earn another precious point. Finally, there was the home game against Spurs, then the trip to Ayresome Park, and by that time the championship trophy was all but on its way to Anfield. As Paisley said, 'it lies between us and Ipswich'. Goals from Lawrenson, Whelan and Dalglish meant that Liverpool won 3-1 and, in the process, clocked up a record that season of never having lost to Spurs in their three encounters – twice in the League, once at Wembley; neither had they been beaten in four duels with Arsenal (two League, two League Cup), while against Ipswich Town they had won two and drawn one of the four matches played. From the first fixture – when they had lost to Wolverhampton – to their final (and 61st), Liverpool had stayed the course, and so had two of their players, because Grobbelaar and Neal had been ever-presents, while Dalglish had missed figuring in the starting line-up only once. Rush and Souness had missed just a handful of matches, and the former had been prominent as a marksman – not least when he hit a hat-trick against Notts. County and scored twice against Swansea in the F.A. Cup and against Birmingham in the League. McDermott had been a marksman more than a dozen times, including a brace of goals against Oulu Palloseura in Europe and against Swansea in the League, in successive matches. He had also hit two goals against Aston Villa and followed up by scoring in the next two games – on both occasions, Ipswich Town had felt the impact of his shooting. Liverpool had made it 10 wins on the trot when they sank Nottingham Forest, while Rush had led the parade of First Division marksmen. For Tottenham Hotspur – and, of course, for Bob Paisley's Liverpool – the season had emphasised just how slender the margin can be between success and failure … because, while Liverpool had achieved a double, Spurs had had to suffer the agony not only of losing at Wembley, but of going out of the European Cup-winners Cup at the semi-final hurdle, as well as having to acknowledge during the final weeks of the season that the League championship, too, was now beyond them.

However, Tottenham still had one last shot in their locker – they were going on from Anfield and returning to Wembley, there to take on London rivals Queen's Park Rangers in the final of the F.A. Cup. Rangers then were in the Second Division, and Spurs were rated firm favourites to win the trophy. It was, as I wrote in the Anfield Review, 'a tantalising prospect' for Tottenham … who, to cap it all, had suffered a spate of injuries in the weeks leading up to the F.A. Cup final. As Bob Paisley conceded: 'Most people would agree that Spurs deserve to claim some reward for their efforts' – then he added: 'We'll settle for a Tottenham success at Wembley, just so long as we get three points today!' Liverpool duly got their three points, Spurs defeated Queen's Park Rangers – though it needed a replay to decide the destination of the F.A. Cup – and the season ended for Bob Paisley and his players with that scoreless draw at Middlesbrough and the knowledge that, yet again, Liverpool had remained the team all the others had to beat.

CHAPTER 15

Bob's Final Bow

ASTON VILLA played a significant part in Bob Paisley's list of memorable moments … there was the championship success on the 40th anniversary of his arrival at Anfield, and another occasion was the last time that Paisley would take his seat in the main stand at Anfield, as Liverpool's manager. That was Saturday, May 7, 1983. Once again, Liverpool had the League Cup in their possession, and once again, they had the championship trophy in their grasp … so, once again, Bob Paisley had steered them to a double, and he was about to bow out on a high note.

Only a couple of weeks before the match against Villa, he had something to say about the business of achieving success. Like this: 'Football is all about winning. It's a fiercely competitive game, and the honours are thinly spread among the 92 League clubs. The fact that Liverpool have scooped up so many of the major prizes during the past decade has prompted some people to say it's time the honours went around a bit more … to which my reply is, "Liverpool permitting!"' This wily old fox of a manager had something else for people to chew upon, too… 'I have gained a great deal of satisfaction – perhaps the greatest satisfaction – from the knowledge that we have achieved our success with arguably the smallest playing squad, numerically, in the club's history. People may talk about the Liverpools of this world being able to splash money around without a second thought. That simply isn't true – and our actions confirm this. Like every other club, we have felt the draught of the recession, and we have had to take action accordingly. One of the ways in which we have helped to balance the budget has been by pruning the playing staff'.

Two of the one-time first-team regulars, Ray Kennedy and Terry McDermott, had moved on; so had reserve-team players such as Howard Gayle – a substitute in a European Cup-tie against Bayern Munich – and Colin Russell, a striker who at one stage had looked set for a lengthy career at Liverpool. Meanwhile, Super-sub David Fairclough had had a spell in American Soccer, and another player, Robbie Savage, had been out on loan at Wrexham. Paisley pointed out, also, that not only had the club kept pace with new demands… 'we have been proving, also, that we have some extremely versatile footballers'. Dalglish, Lawrenson and Johnston, for example, had slotted into various roles as the need arose. Paisley concluded: 'So what has pleased me as much as anything is the fact that we can still maintain a high standard, despite making necessary and sensible economies – and I firmly believe we are equipped to carry on challenging for honours'. Yes, as he prepared to bow out, he knew he was leaving Liverpool in pretty good shape – as his successor, Joe Fagan, was about to demonstrate.

Liverpool were on the verge of celebrating a 14th League-championship success and rarely, if ever, could a club have coasted home so comfortably. The Anfield club had been sitting on top of the First Division table almost every Saturday since taking over the leadership – and that was way back on September 25, 1982. Liverpool had been top dogs for 31 Saturdays out of 37 (and remember that there were no League tables on the first Saturday of the season). It was in total contrast to the situation the previous season, when – after seven matches – 11 other clubs stood between Liverpool and the top of the table. Towards the end of September, 1981, when Liverpool were looking up at the 11 clubs above them, title talk had been muted – but Paisley's team had come storming through to triumph. Towards the end of September, 1982, Liverpool had won five and drawn two games out of seven, and with 17 points they sat astride the table, looking down on everyone else … as they were to do through most of the campaign. After a dozen matches, in fact, they were never caught and, indeed, at one stage they had stretched their lead at the head of the table into double figures. It was recorded that 'Manchester United and Watford have gamely stuck to our heels, but there will be little significance now in our visit to Vicarage Road for the final match of the season, while United had to concede eventually that their best hope of success was in a cup competition'.

Once again, Liverpool had totalled more matches than most – 59, to be precise – and this time out, the goals had fairly flowed for Rush and Dalglish. Rushy? – Two at Swansea, two at Ipswich in the League-Milk Cup, FOUR in a 5-0 thrashing of Everton – and this one at Goodison Park – plus a hat-trick against Coventry City, another one against Notts County, and a brace of goals against Brighton … not to mention the solo goals in more than a dozen other matches. As for Dalglish, it took him 17 games to get going; then he hit two goals against Brighton and two more against Spurs, to take his tally to seven in half a dozen outings overall. He struck a hat-trick against Manchester City and scored twice against Notts. County, to clock up half a dozen goals in four outings, and he was a two-goal marksman against Stoke, with four other 'singles' before that match.

As a team, Liverpool had viewed the season as one of four stages, in total. In each of these stages they had reeled off a string of results without defeat – initially, nine matches unbeaten (two dozen goals scored, just seven conceded); then a scoring spree which produced 28 goals (three conceded) in a run of 10 games; then (after a 1-0 defeat at Norwich) an unbeaten sequence of 14 matches in which the side rattled in 35 goals while conceding only 10. The fourth stage of the season brought another 10-match run during which Liverpool scored 23 goals and conceded only half a dozen. And by that time, the League-Milk Cup was once more adorning the Anfield trophy room while the championship trophy was being polished in readiness for the handing-over ceremony. Dalglish claimed the Player-of-the-Year award, courtesy of the votes from his fellow professionals; Rush wound up as the Young-Player-of-the-Year; Dalglish then followed up by winning the sportswriters' Footballer-of-the-Year award; and Bob Paisley? – Well … he was the recipient of a Merit Award and set to claim the Manager-of-the-Year award for the sixth time in eight seasons. A staggering achievement, by any standards.

Liverpool had kicked off by defeating West Brom at Anfield, and by mid-January they were completing a League double over Albion. They had also done the double over Arsenal, Manchester City, Notts County and Swansea City, and as the season came to its close they were in line for a double over Aston Villa at Anfield and at Watford in their final game. In two matches there had been nail-biting moments: 4-3 against Nottingham Forest, 3-3 against Southampton.

Liverpool's players had made history – and not for the first time – with their League-Milk Cup win at Wembley, because they had become the first club to make it a hat-trick of successes in this competition, as they staved off the challenge from another pot-hunting club, Manchester United … although that final had gone to extra time. Bob Paisley made another little bit of history, too, when he became the first manager to go up the steps and collect the trophy. It was Paisley who presented Kenny Dalglish with his Player-of-the-Year award, and Paisley who, in claiming a Merit Award (for outstanding services to football), followed in the footsteps of previous winners Bill Shankly, Matt Busby, Tom Finney and Bobby Charlton. And – appropriately – it was presented to Bob by a former Anfield scoring idol, Roger Hunt. One way and another, Liverpool had almost scooped the pool … but there had been a couple of exceptions; because they had suffered keen disappointment in the F.A. Cup and European Cup.

In the F.A. Cup, Liverpool had taken their team of all the talents to Ewood Park at the beginning of January and, with goals from Rush and Hodgson, scored a 2-1 win; in the fourth round, a home draw against Stoke City brought a 2-0 victory (goals from Dalglish and Rush); and with another home draw, against Brighton (First Division strugglers at the time), Liverpool seemed to be paving the way for a return to Wembley. But Brighton rode their luck at Anfield and, with a fighting display, shook the home fans by winning 2-1. Substitute Craig Johnston's goal was too little, too late. If there was a consolation for Paisley, it was the knowledge that Brighton marched on to Wembley and took Manchester United to a replay.

The European Cup appeared to be brimming with promise, too, as Liverpool embarked upon the trail with a trip to Dundalk ... who suffered a 4-1 setback on Irish soil as the former Home Farm starlet Ronnie Whelan chipped in with two goals (the others came from Rush and Hodgson). Of course, the return game was a formality – yet it took a goal from Whelan to win it. The second round also paired Liverpool with what seemed easy opposition; the Finnish club, JK Helsinki ... but when Paisley's team travelled for the first leg, they came unstuck, and travelled back home somewhat subdued, after a 1-0 defeat. There were no mistakes in the return encounter, however – at Anfield, a 5-0 scoreline in Liverpool's favour said it all. And so, at that stage, it was looking good.

Two goals from Alan Kennedy, one apiece from Neal, Dalglish and Johnston did the damage and took Liverpool into a third-round tie against the relatively-unrated Poles of Widzew Lodz. It did indeed appear as if Liverpool could be well and truly on their way to another triumph in the European Cup. Before meeting the Poles in March, however, there was the little matter of the League-Milk Cup, and in the space of four days at the beginning of October, Liverpool had to tackle Ipswich Town twice – each time at Portman Road. The League game came first, and it ended with the first defeat in 10 matches, by the only goal of the game. It came after Liverpool had beaten Nottingham Forest 4-3 and drawn 3-3 with Luton Town (both games were played at Anfield), and after they had beaten Dundalk away, Swansea City 3-0 away, Southampton 5-0 at Anfield and Dundalk in the European return.

Having lost to Ipswich on October 2, Liverpool went back to Portman Road on October 5 for the Milk Cup test, and this time they ran out winners by the odd goal in three (both their goals came from Ian Rush). There were mixed results then, up to the second leg of the Cup-tie at Anfield, where Ipswich were beaten 2-0, and where Brighton went down 3-1 in the League. The Goodison debacle, with Liverpool hammering Everton 5-0, came immediately before another home tie in the Milk Cup, against Rotherham United – who were managed by former Anfield favourite Emlyn Hughes. Emlyn had been back to Anfield as a member of the Wolves team, but this was the first time he had walked through the door as 'the boss' of the opposition. He admitted that on the two occasions he had played at Anfield for Wolves, he hadn't enjoyed it – because he'd finished on the losing end; now, he admitted that since he arrived at Rotherham, 'everything I have done has followed the Liverpool pattern. Everything I learned in the game, I learned when I was at Liverpool – and in 13 years I should have learned something!'

Rotherham had knocked out promotion favourites Queen's Park Rangers, but Hughes confessed that when it came to summing up Liverpool, that was a different kettle of fish. 'There simply isn't any formula for beating them'. And he was right, because while Rotherham gave almost as good as they got, at the end of the night it was Liverpool who had won the match, though only by a single goal. The match-winner: Craig Johnston. And so it was on to round four, with yet another home tie, this time against Norwich City.

The Canaries were conquered, with goals from Lawrenson and substitute David Fairclough, and that victory took Liverpool on to a fifth-round meeting with West Ham ... once more, the venue was Anfield. It was a tricky tie, but goals from Hodgson and Souness ensured a 2-1 win for the home side and a semi-final date with their near neighbours from Burnley. Once again, Hodgson and Souness were on the mark, with a third goal coming from Neal, so Liverpool went to Turf Moor for the second leg confident of reaching Wembley. They were not to be disappointed, either, although Burnley scored the only goal of the return game, and by that time Liverpool were looking ahead to the final days of February and the beginning of March. Straight after their success against Burnley came that shock defeat by Brighton in the F.A. Cup at Anfield, but Liverpool recovered by drawing 1-1 against Manchester United at Old Trafford before embarking upon their European Cup safari once again.

Widzew Lodz were not exactly a household name, and Liverpool could reaonably expect to get a result – either a draw or an outright victory – at the first time of trying. Instead, they returned home having failed to score and having conceded a couple of goals. Now they had everything to play for, at Anfield – they had it all to do. Bob Paisley spelled it out for the fans and for his team... Widzew Lodz were better than Slask Wroclaw and stood comparison with Dynamo Dresden. In Poland, Liverpool had weathered the first 15 minutes of an attacking barrage, and as half-time approached, they were feeling pretty confident. Then, as Paisley said, 'came the moments of disaster...' He insisted, though: 'Dwelling on mistakes does no good – we must have a positive attitude and go for goals'. He reminded everyone that Liverpool had overcome before, and he instanced matches against Bruges ... 'they caught us cold and scored twice' ... and against AZ'67 Alkmaar ... 'a nail-biting affair as the teams came towards the final whistle with the scoreline 2-2 on the night and 4-4 overall; but, in the dying minutes, we claimed the decisive goal'. It boiled down to the fact that Liverpool had to win 3-0 inside 90 minutes, or 2-0 to force extra time. He urged his players to 'prove brave enough, bold enough and good enough to retrieve the situation. It's actions, not words which will count'. A stirring message, and a challenge to his team, without a doubt. However, Paisley did warn of the consequences should the Poles manage to score a goal.

His warning turned out to have been utterly justified, because although Phil Neal scored from the penalty spot with the game barely 15 minutes old, Widzew Lodz also put one in Liverpool's net, so that by half-time the score was 1-1 and 3-1 to the Poles on aggregate. By the time that the game was into its final 10 minutes most of the home supporters had just about given up the ghost, yet the players continued to heed their manager's words as they carried on battling to retrieve the desperate situation. Ten minutes left – and there was a goal from Rush ... could Liverpool, somehow, still do it? – More minutes ticked away, and there were 60 seconds on the clock for normal time – then Hodgson scored, to make it three for Liverpool. But it was all over, bar the shouting, because while Paisley's team had been pegging away, the Poles had snatched a second goal and so when time ran out, they claimed victory by an aggregate scoreline of 4-3. The road to the European Cup final had been closed for Liverpool.

Now it was the League-Milk Cup and/or the championship again. And straight after the blow of defeat in the Champions Cup Liverpool had to face Everton at Anfield and then travel to Brighton, to see what they could do against their conquerors in the F.A. Cup. It was 0-0 in the first encounter, 2-2 at the Goldstone Ground; which took Liverpool on to meet Manchester United four days later at Wembley. Twelve months previously, Liverpool and Spurs had slugged it out during a final which had gone to extra time; and this time round there was to be a repeat performance, with Ronnie Whelan, the man whose goals had paved the way against Tottenham, once more playing a key role in the outcome. Ironically, Whelan had been tipped to land at Manchester United before he opted for Anfield. In 1981, Liverpool had beaten West Ham (in a replay); in 1982 it had been Spurs (at Wembley) ... and now it was Manchester United who barred the way to a memorable hat-trick.

Not surprisingly, it was a keenly-contested final – Liverpool-United duels always have that extra spice about them – and at half-time you might well have laid a small bet that the winners would come from Manchester, not Merseyside, because Liverpool were a goal down. The marksman: Norman Whiteside. And with just quarter of an hour remaining, the odds looked increasingly on the trophy going to Manchester ... then Liverpool fans were in full cry as Alan Kennedy beat 'keeper Gary Bailey.

Suddenly it was Liverpool who had their tails up and United who were striving to make their presence felt; but there were no more goals during the course of the 90 minutes, and so it was a case of extra time. While Grobbelaar's goal was to remain intact during the next 30 minutes, Bailey was to concede one more; and the man who might well have become a team-mate was the villain of the piece. Ninety-eight minutes had gone, and Whelan gained possession; then the Irishman sent in a curling chip shot which had United's 'keeper leaping despairingly in the attempt to make contact with the ball. But he was a mile away from preventing it from looping over him and into the net. And so Liverpool completed the hat-trick while, at the same time, their fans celebrated what might be termed revenge for that 1977 F.A. Cup final defeat by what was then Tommy

Docherty's team – a defeat which had denied Bob Paisley and his men what would indeed have been an historic treble.

There were two voices raised in praise of Paisley and his team … one of them being the voice of a Liverpudlian who had become the manager of Manchester United; the other who was in charge of team affairs across the way from Old Trafford… John Benson, the manager of Manchester City. Ron Atkinson first: 'Bob is the greatest manager of all time. He took over a superb club and team, but he has taken them forward to even greater achievements…' And this from John Benson: 'I watched Liverpool beating Manchester United at Wembley, and even from those televised highlights it was clear to see what a great and complete team they are. The record of their manager, Bob Paisley, is second to none; he has swept up the honours at home and abroad with a string of achievements that will be almost impossible to beat'.

And what of Liverpool, as they saw Paisley sign off with the championship trophy and League-Milk Cup? – From chairman John Smith came this unstinting tribute: 'Our final League game at Anfield marks the end of one era and the beginning of another, because this is the last time Bob Paisley will take his seat in the stand as Liverpool's manager … yet he will still be serving the club in another capacity (as a director). My outstanding memory of Bob is of the day he was appointed manager. As we chatted at my home, it was something of an emotional experience, for what shone through most was Bob's unswerving loyalty to the cause of Liverpool F.C. He was prepared to take on what he knew must be a difficult task but, as ever, he was committed to giving 100 per cent, to the club'.

Smith himself had once told me that for him, 'Liverpool Football Club is almost a religion'; and now he was saying of Paisley: 'I cannot stress too highly the quality of the man himself, for he has applied the wisdom of his experience to the job and, where others might have been tempted to bask in the glory, he has never allowed success to go to his head'. It was a tribute echoed by a man who, in his own time as a team boss, was to suffer some taunts from the tabloids after initially having achieved considerable success… Graham Taylor, whose career took off at Watford, thrived at Aston Villa, and foundered with England and Wolves. Taylor's Watford chased Liverpool home in the championship race, after having graduated to the First Division, and he reflected: 'What capped it for me was beating Liverpool in Bob Paisley's last game as a manager (this match took place at Vicarage Road, after the Aston Villa game at Anfield). I kept the team sheet, and I still have it at home. It seems a little thing, but if there was a man I did admire from a distance, it was Bob Paisley. I thought he was a very knowledgeable and shrewd man about his people and football'.

From Mark Lawrenson, whom he signed for £900,000, came this reflection:

'He was like my grand-dad, I suppose. He was probably the shrewdest person I ever met in football. Half the time, if you didn't know who he was, you'd think he was just a guy who worked at the ground. There were no airs and graces about him'. On the subject of Paisley as a communicator: 'He was the master of the unfinished sentence'. Indeed, he was … very often, Bob would conclude what he was saying with the remark 'and that…' and leave you to work out the meaning. Lawrenson, whom I found to be an extremely articulate person, easy-going and approachable, said that at some team meetings you would wonder exactly what Paisley meant – 'but his message managed to get through. He had his own kind of language, if you will'. Lawrenson also echoed what Nessie Shankly said – that Paisley thought before he spoke. Usually, he saved his post-match inquest until the Monday – 'I think he felt there was a danger of things being said in the heat of the moment, after a bad game. He'd like to think things through'.

From a football fan who lived in Barnsley, a letter to a national newspaper demonstrated that Paisley's Liverpool had admirers a fair distance from Anfield. The fan wrote: 'I still remember Arsenal's Chapman … the pomp and class of Real Madrid in the late 1950's … the brash confidence of Borussia Moenchengladbach … the sophistication of Ajax. I am the first to acknowledge that there have been a lot of good sides; but has there ever been a team the equal of Liverpool … how on earth does the Anfield club keep it up? – Week by week, season after season, they are in the middle of battles for cups, championships or honours of some kind. There is truly something magical about Liverpool; something that puts them above all others. Liverpool are the finest football unit of all time'. Well, Bob Paisley did say that he wanted his team to do the talking for him.

CHAPTER 16

And a Postscript

BOB PAISLEY talking: 'As a racing enthusiast who enjoys the occasional flutter, I can appreciate the feelings of the punter who beats the bookies when the horse he's backed gets its nose past the winning post first. As a football manager, I can look at the odds quoted by the bookmakers for the First Division championship – and put them to the back of my mind'. That statement came at a time, not long before he retired from management, when these were the title odds quotes by the bookies: Liverpool 7-4; Manchester United 5-1; Ipswich Town 6-1; Manchester City, having lost Trevor Francis, were outsiders at 25-1. Paisley said that it was flattering to see his club installed as favourites for the title – 'I suppose this is only to be expected, after our spate of successes during the past years' – yet being installed as favourites 'makes it harder, if anything, for us to live up to that rating'. He wasn't wrong there, either.

He was realistic enough to recognise that at the start, every club kicked off even in the race … which was not the same as saying that every club had the same chance of winning. He recalled a season when Liverpool made what he called 'a stuttering start and didn't get a grip of things until after the turn of the year. Three points for a win produced some surprises and, for us, we had to adapt as we went along. I recognised the signs, as players tried to pace the game to suit themselves.' And when it came to the championship of the First Division – 'Above all, consistency is the name of the game'. After Liverpool had been acclaimed champions for the 13th time in their history, Paisley called it 'the proudest moment of my career, because it was the hardest of all our title wins. We changed the team about, had to bring in new players'.

Succinctly, Liverpool's manager observed: 'The hardest part of this job is producing them at the right moment'. No-one knew better than this man what it took to produce a team which could go the distance in the championship race – not just once, but season after season. As Paisley took his final bow, he admitted: 'I've tried to imagine just how I shall feel, as I walk into the dressing-room after the match … but I'll know for certain when that moment comes'. In the meantime, and typical of the man, 'I have no doubts about one thing: so many people have made this job easier for me to do, at various times during the past nine years, that I wonder now why I even hesitated about taking it on. In fact, I have come to realise that the easiest thing about the job was the way that people went out of their way to be of genuine assistance. As for the hardest thing during my time as manager … that's an easy one to answer. Quite simply, it was the decision to pack the job in!'

Possibly Paisley remembered that after Bill Shankly had refused to be talked out of quitting as Liverpool's manager, there came a time when Bill appeared to be something of a lost soul, a man in limbo; as if he were wondering what on earth he had really done. Yet Paisley, having reflected upon matters, accepted that 'everything – good and bad – has to come to an end, sooner or later'. He said, somewhat wryly: 'You cannot please all of the people all of the time, and I know that I haven't always suited everyone in this city, or even at this club. Fortunately, the people who from time to time have been critical of my actions turned out to be very much in a minority – and I'd like to think that I've never reached the stage where the critics and I were never going to be on speaking terms again!' Asked what being a Freeman of the City of Liverpool involved, Paisley answered, jokingly: 'In my case, being given a free transfer!' Then he added, being serious: 'I am very sensible of all the honours which have come my way while I have lived and worked in Liverpool; and I am not merely paying lip service to this club when I say I regard most of the honours as being for Liverpool F.C. as well as for myself'.

He referred to 'the diffidence I felt, when I was asked to follow Bill Shankly', and declared: 'There have been times when I felt, sincerely, that the players and the staff were making the job look ridiculously easy for me'. Maybe they did make it look that way – but Paisley was the guiding light.

It was Ronnie Moran, one of Paisley's henchmen, who offered the opinion that Bob had been 20 or 30 years 'ahead of his time' when he forecast that the day would dawn when footballers employed agents and carried advertising on their shirts. It was, in fact, away back in September, 1978, that Liverpool's manager took a close look at what had been going on in the transfer market during the close season – and wondered out loud if 'we'll see the day when a wealthy gentleman from the Middle East will offer a club a share in an oil well, in return for a star player'. Even as Paisley dubbed this 'a flight of fancy', he was also saying: 'I wonder…' At that time, Tottenham Hotspur had splashed £700,000 on two stars from Argentina – Osvaldo Ardiles and Ricardo Villa – while they had also paid Fulham £240,000 for defender John Lacey. Ipswich had signed Dutchman Arnold Muhren for £140,000, Alan Kennedy had arrived at Anfield from Newcastle, who had paid an estimated quarter of a million to Nottingham Forest for striker Peter Withe.

In signing defender Paul Futcher from Luton Town, Manchester City had taken their spending past the £550,000 mark as they also signed Futcher's twin brother, Ron, plus Colin Viljoen from Ipswich. And as the transfer merry-go-round continued, Paisley talked about the money involved. 'People ask me how I think transfer fees will go and, frankly, I have to tell them I don't know; but the thoughts of what might happen can be a bit frightening, at times, and I wouldn't bet against the day when we see a player moving in a straight million-pound deal between one British club and another'. Paisley harked back to his own arrival at Liverpool – 'I cost a £10 signing-on fee' – and to the same era when Arsenal had just paid Wolves £14,000 for Bryn Jones. 'The event staggered Soccer', he said. 'When Jones didn't make an immediate hit, it was suggested the massive fee was worrying him into loss of form'.

As for Liverpool, they splashed £13,000 on Albert Stubbins, and as Paisley talked about his former team-mate he declared: 'In those days, people said it was like a millstone around a player's neck … today, it would make scarcely a ripple in the transfer market. When Liverpool sold Kevin Keegan, the size of the fee was regarded as sensational … yet we were only too happy to go out and sign a player who, in our opinion, could do the job for us as effectively as Kevin had'.

Paisley again: 'If someone had talked about a half-million-pound transfer only a few years ago, most people would have smiled sceptically. But not any more. Sponsorship is playing an ever-increasing part in football, and lotteries are also raising money. So there may be more cash available for signing players. It's fair to say that big clubs such as Liverpool know when they go for a player that the asking price will be high, because they are considered able to afford it. That doesn't mean we always agree! But the transfer trend is still pointing in an upward direction…' And that was where, in his 'flight of fancy', Bob Paisley wondered out loud about someone offering a share in an oil well, in return for a Soccer star.

However, even Bob Paisley didn't foresee the day when Roy Evans would be asking Liverpool to spend £8.5 million upon one footballer. And shortly after Bob had died, and Liverpool were back on course to resume their quest for honours, chief executive Peter Robinson was able to look forward, as well as back upon what was termed 'Liverpool's glorious domination of the championship in the 1980's' which, the writer said, had become 'faded but not fully diminished by recent seasons of unusual uncertainty'. Robinson reflected, as Liverpool chased Manchester United and Newcastle United for the Premiership title in the spring of 1996, that 'we are confident the blip is now behind us. The plans we have laid during the past couple of years, both short and long-term, are coming to fruition. We have a good squad of players and will have the resources to compete for other top players as and when they become available. We can see no reason why we should not, once again, be among the successful clubs fighting for the major prizes. We never thought the great days had gone for ever – our support was maintained, not just here but throughout the world. We knew that as long as we had that support and confidence, things could be put right again'.

Robinson admitted that 'it's going to be increasingly difficult for any club to dominate in the future as we did in the past. I have always said you can't win anything if you haven't got good players and a good manager. Certainly you can't win anything with a good administrator and bad players'. And Robinson himself was regarded as one of the finest administrators in football. His reference to Liverpool's domination in the past took in the eras of Dalglish, Fagan ... and, of course, Paisley and Shankly.

Speaking as someone who, like Paisley, had given sterling service to the club since his arrival in 1965, Robinson was able to say, from first-hand knowledge and with quiet confidence, that 'there's a buzz about the place again with the players, management, staff and supporters ... the old feeling is back at Anfield. The supporters never thought this situation was beyond us again, and the buzz suggests that it's just like it used to be'. That was a verdict which would have brought a knowing smile to the face of that wily old fox, Bob Paisley.